The Ultimate AZ-900 Flash Cards Collection

Your Key to Success in the Azure Cloud

2nd Edition

Table of Contents

Course Introduction 9

Introduction 9

Course Objectives 9

Why AZ-900? 9

Importance of this Certification 10

What you will learn in this course? 10

Who is this course for? 12

Career Growth with this Course 12

Prerequisites 13

Recertification 14

Basic Concepts 15

Azure Backup and Disaster Recovery 22

Authentication 26

Authorization 29

Azure Cost Management 32

Azure Pricing 35

Azure AI Services 38

Azure Database 42

Azure Support 46

Azure Data and Analytics 50

Azure Networking Services 55

Azure Security Services 59

Azure Compute Services 64

Azure Web Services 69

Azure Mobile Services 72

Azure Storage 75

Azure Monitoring and Management 80

Azure Internet of Things (IoT) 85

How to Interact with Azure 90

Azure Marketplace 94

Azure Physical Infrastructure 99

Azure Management Infrastructure 104

Azure Container Instances (ACI) 109

Azure Core Solutions and Management Tools 112

Azure Zero Trust Model 117

Azure Defense in Depth 120

Distributed Denial-of-Service Attacks (DDoS) 126

Azure Key Vault 130

Azure Information Protection (AIP) 134

Advanced Threat Protection (ATP) 138

Azure Sentinel 142

Azure Dedicated Host 145

Privacy, Compliance, and Trust 149

Secure Azure Resources with RBAC 153

Secure Azure Resources with RBAC 157

Compliance 161

Azure Government Cloud 164

Azure Privacy 168

Azure Trust 172

Azure Pricing Factors 176

Total Cost of Ownership (TCO) Calculator 180

Best Practices for Minimizing Azure Costs 183

Managing and Deploying Azure Resources 187

Azure Resource Manager (ARM) 191

Structure of ARM Templates 194

Working with ARM Templates 198

Azure Arc 201

Azure Portal 204

Azure Plan 208

Service Level Agreements (SLAs) in Azure 212

Azure Authentication 216

Azure Cloud Shell 220

Azure PowerShell 224

Azure Identity Services 227

Traffic Manager and Azure DNS 233

About Our Products 237

Microsoft Certifications

Microsoft Azure Certifications are industry-recognized credentials that validate your technical Cloud skills and expertise while assisting your career growth. These are one of the most valuable IT certifications since Azure has established an overwhelming growth rate in the public cloud market. Even with several tough competitors such as Amazon Web Services, Google Cloud Engine, and Rackspace, Azure will be the dominant public cloud platform today, with an astounding collection of proprietary services that continues to grow.

In this certification, we will discuss cloud concepts where we will learn the core benefits of using Azure, like high availability, scalability, etc. We will talk about the Azure Architecture in which cloud resources are put together to work at best; Azure Compute, where you will learn how to run applications in Azure; Networking, in which the discussion is on how Azure resources communicate with each other; Storage, where you put all of your data and have different ways of storing it. We will also cover databases used for data storage, their efficient retrieval as per demand, and ensuring that the users have the right access to the resources. Also, we will counter some complex scenarios with their solutions. We will have discussions on important topics like Security, which makes Azure the best secure choice for your applications and functions; Privacy, Compliance, and Trust which make sure services ensure privacy; and how you stay compliant with standards. As well as, pricing in Azure to stay ahead on cost.

AZ-900 is the first certification of Microsoft Azure, the foundational certificate in Azure. After this certification, you can prove to the world that you are proficient and have the credibility to reach the highest point of your professional life.

Value of Azure Certifications

Microsoft emphasizes sound conceptual knowledge of its entire platform and hands-on experience with the Azure infrastructure and its many unique and complex components and services.

For Individuals

- Demonstrate your expertise in designing, deploying, and operating highly available, cost-effective, and secured applications on Microsoft Azure.
- Gain recognition and visibility of your proven skills and proficiency with Azure.
- Earn tangible benefits such as access to the Microsoft Certified Community, getting invited to Microsoft Certification Appreciation Receptions and Lounges, obtaining Microsoft Certification Practice Exam Voucher and Digital Badge for certification validation, and Microsoft Certified Logo usage.
- Foster credibility with your employer and peers.

For Employers

- Identify skilled professionals to lead IT initiatives with Cloud technologies.
- To implement your workloads and projects on the Azure platform, reduce risks and costs.
- Increase customer satisfaction.

Types of Certifications

Role-based Certification

- *Fundamental* - Validates overall understanding of the Azure Cloud.
- *Associate-* Technical role-based certifications. No pre-requisite is required.
- *Expert-* Highest level technical role-based certification.

About Microsoft Certified: <u>Microsoft Azure Fundamentals</u>

Exam Questions	Case study, short answer, repeated answer, MCQs
Number of Questions	40-60
Time to Complete	85 minutes
Exam Fee	99 USD

Candidates for AZ-900 exam should have the foundational knowledge of cloud services and how those services are provided with Microsoft Azure. The exam is intended for candidates who are just beginning to work with cloud-based solutions and services or are new to Azure. The Azure Fundamentals exam is an opportunity to prove knowledge of cloud concepts, Azure services, Azure workloads, security and privacy in Azure, and Azure pricing and support. Candidates should be familiar with general technology concepts, including networking, storage, compute, application support, and application development. Azure Fundamentals can be used to prepare for other Azure role-based or specialty certifications, but it is not a prerequisite for any of them.

This exam measures your ability to accomplish the following technical tasks:

• Describe cloud concepts	25-30%
• Describe Azure architecture and services	35-40%
• Describe Azure management and governance	30-35%

Recommended Knowledge

- Identify the benefits and considerations of using cloud services
- Describe the differences between categories of cloud services
- Describe the differences between types of cloud computing
- Describe the core Azure architectural components
- Describe core resources available in Azure
- Describe core solutions available in Azure
- Describe Azure management tools
- Describe Azure security features
- Describe Azure network security
- Describe core Azure identity services
- Describe Azure governance features
- Describe privacy and compliance resources
- Describe methods for planning and managing costs
- Describe Azure Service Level Agreements (SLAs) and service lifecycles

All the required information is included in this Study Guide.

	Domain	Percentage
Domain 1	Describe cloud concepts	25-30%
Domain 2	Describe Azure architecture and services	35-40%
Domain 3	Describe Azure management and governance	30-35%

Course Introduction

Introduction

AZ-900 is the first certification of Microsoft Azure, the foundational certificate in Azure. After this certification, you can prove to the world that you are proficient and have the credibility to reach the highest point of your professional life. This course validates your basic understanding of cloud services and how Microsoft Azure provides them. It covers the basics of Azure cloud computing, including core Azure services, subscription management, security, privacy, compliance, and trust.

Course Objectives

- **Cloud Concepts:** Understand the fundamentals of cloud computing, including deployment models, service models, and the benefits of cloud services.
- **Azure Services**: Explore core Azure services and products, learning how they contribute to building and managing applications in the cloud.
- **Azure Pricing and Support:** Gain insights into Azure pricing models, Service Level Agreements (SLA), and how to manage costs effectively.
- **Azure Governance and Compliance:** Learn about implementing and managing Azure policies, Role-Based Access Control (RBAC), and monitoring in Azure.
- **Azure Identity, Privacy, and Data Protection:** Dive into Microsoft Entra ID, Multi-Factor Authentication (MFA), and data protection features in Azure.
- **Azure Solutions**: Explore Internet of Things (IoT), Artificial Intelligence (AI), and Big Data and Analytics solutions in Azure.

Why AZ-900?

- It serves as a foundational certification for individuals new to Azure.
- It provides a broad overview of key cloud concepts and Azure services.
- It prepares you for more advanced Azure certifications.

Importance of this Certification

The AZ-900 certification holds significance as it establishes a foundational understanding of cloud computing principles and introduces key Azure services. Recognized by Microsoft, this certification validates individuals' knowledge of fundamental concepts such as cloud concepts, core Azure services, security, compliance, privacy, and pricing. It serves as an entry point for those pursuing a career in cloud computing, providing a valuable credential for job seekers and professionals seeking to broaden their skill set. Additionally, for business and technical decision-makers, the AZ-900 certification offers insights into Azure's capabilities, aiding in informed decision-making about cloud adoption. Overall, the certification is a recognized benchmark that enhances career opportunities and lays the groundwork for pursuing more advanced Azure certifications.

What you will learn in this course?

In the Microsoft Azure Fundamentals (AZ-900) course, you will acquire a foundational understanding of cloud computing and Microsoft Azure services. Here is an overview of what you will learn in this course:

Cloud Concepts

- Understand the basic principles of cloud computing.
- Differentiate between various cloud deployment models, such as public, private, and hybrid clouds.
- Explore service models, including Infrastructure as a Service (IaaS), Platform as a Service (PaaS), and Software as a Service (SaaS).

Azure Services Overview:

- Explore key Azure services and products.
- Understand the core architectural components of Azure.
- Learn how to use Azure solutions and management tools.

Azure Pricing and Support:

- Gain insights into Azure pricing models and factors influencing costs.
- Understand Service Level Agreements (SLA) and the service lifecycle.
- Learn how to manage Azure costs effectively.

Azure Governance and Compliance:

- Implement and manage Azure policies for resource organization and control.
- Understand Role-Based Access Control (RBAC) for managing access to Azure resources.
- Explore monitoring and reporting tools in Azure.

Azure Identity, Privacy, and Data Protection:

- Dive into Microsoft Entra ID (Azure AD) and its role in identity management.
- Explore features like Multi-Factor Authentication (MFA) and Identity Protection.
- Understand data protection features in Azure, including Azure Information Protection.

Azure Solutions:

- Explore key Azure solutions, including Internet of Things (IoT), Artificial Intelligence (AI), and Big Data and Analytics.
- Understand how these solutions can be applied to real-world scenarios.

Azure Management Tools:

- Navigate the Azure Portal and perform tasks using Azure PowerShell and Azure CLI.
- Understand Azure Resource Manager (ARM) templates for infrastructure as code.
- Explore Azure Monitor and Microsoft Defender for Cloud for management and monitoring.

Security, Privacy, Compliance, and Trust:

- Learn about Microsoft Defender for Cloud for threat protection.
- Understand the role of Azure Key Vault in secure key management.
- Explore compliance features in Azure, including GDPR and other standards.

By the end of this course, you will have a solid foundation in cloud computing concepts and a practical understanding of how to use Microsoft Azure services

effectively. Additionally, you'll be well-prepared to take the AZ-900 exam, earning a certification that validates your Azure fundamentals knowledge.

Who is this course for?

The Microsoft Azure AZ-900 exam and its associated course, Microsoft Azure Fundamentals, are designed for individuals who are new to Azure and cloud computing and want to build a foundational understanding of Microsoft's cloud services. This course is ideal for:

IT Professionals: Those who are exploring cloud technologies and want to understand the basics of Azure services. This can include individuals in roles such as system administrators, network administrators, and other IT roles.

Developers: Developers who are getting started with cloud development and need to understand how Azure services can be used to build, deploy, and manage applications in the cloud.

Business Decision Makers: Non-technical professionals, such as business analysts or managers, who need to make informed decisions about adopting cloud services and want a foundational understanding of Azure.

Students and Educators: Students pursuing a career in IT or individuals teaching IT-related courses can benefit from this course to ensure they have a solid understanding of fundamental cloud concepts and Azure services.

Anyone Interested in Cloud Computing: Individuals who are curious about cloud computing in general and want to gain knowledge and skills in using Azure services.

Career Growth with this Course

The impact of obtaining the Microsoft Azure Fundamentals (AZ-900) certification on salary increment can vary based on several factors, including your current job role, the industry you're in, geographical location, level of experience, and overall demand for cloud-related skills in your region. Here are some general considerations:

Career Advancement: Earning a certification like AZ-900 can contribute to career advancement, making you a more competitive candidate for roles related

to cloud computing and Microsoft Azure. With career progression, salary increments are often a natural outcome.

As per Payscale, the annual average compensation of a cloud solutions architect in the United States is approximately $128,000. Starting out in the field, an individual should anticipate making about $85,000; with experience, this can increase to $170,000 or higher in 2024.

Industry Demand: The demand for cloud skills, including those related to Microsoft Azure, is generally high. Organizations are increasingly adopting cloud technologies, and professionals with relevant certifications may be sought after, potentially leading to better compensation.

Negotiation Power: Certifications can enhance your negotiating power during salary discussions. Employers often value certifications as they demonstrate a commitment to professional development and a certain level of expertise.

Market Trends: Keep an eye on market trends and salary surveys specific to your industry and location. Researching average salaries for roles related to Azure or cloud computing in your area can provide insights into potential salary increments.

Job Role Specifics: If your current or desired role involves significant use of Microsoft Azure services, the AZ-900 certification can be particularly beneficial. Specialized roles often come with higher salaries, and certifications can contribute to your suitability for such positions.

Advanced Certifications: While AZ-900 is an entry-level certification, pursuing more advanced Azure certifications (e.g., Azure Administrator, Azure Developer, or Azure Solutions Architect) can further increase your earning potential. Advanced certifications are often associated with more specialized and higher-paying roles.

Prerequisites

There is no prior certification required for this course however, Microsoft recommends some general skills and knowledge that may be beneficial before taking the AZ-900 course:

Familiarity with basic IT concepts: A general understanding of basic IT concepts, such as networking, storage, and computing, can be helpful.

Basic understanding of cloud computing: While not mandatory, having a basic awareness of cloud computing concepts will make it easier to grasp the content covered in the course.

Experience using internet browsers: The course materials and labs may involve using web-based interfaces, so familiarity with internet browsers is beneficial.

Recertification

The specific recertification requirements can vary depending on the certification track and the policies set by Microsoft. Here are some general points regarding recertification:

Certification Validity Period: Many Microsoft certifications, including the Azure certifications, have a validity period (usually two years). After this period, the certification may expire.

Recertification Exams: To maintain certification, individuals may need to pass a recertification exam or take a specific set of exams. Microsoft may update the certification exams to reflect changes in technology and services.

Basic Concepts

Flash Card # 1
Service Categories:
IaaS (Infrastructure as a Service)
PaaS (Platform as a Service)
SaaS (Software as a Service)

Flash Card # 2
Cloud Deployment Models:
Public cloud: Resources shared with other users, accessed over the internet. Offers scalability and cost-effectiveness.
Private cloud: Resources dedicated to a single organization, deployed on-premises or with a hosting provider. Offers security and control.
Hybrid cloud: Combines public and private clouds, allowing data and applications to flow between them. Provides flexibility and choice.

Flash Card # 3
Microsoft Azure
Microsoft Azure is a cloud computing platform that provides a wide range of services, including virtual computing, storage, networking, and analytics, allowing users to build, deploy, and manage applications through Microsoft's global network of data centers.

Flash Card # 4
What is Cloud Computing?
Cloud computing is a technology model that enables ubiquitous, on-demand access to a shared pool of configurable computing resources (e.g., networks,

servers, storage, applications) that can be rapidly provisioned and released
with minimal management effort.

Flash Card #5
Cloud Benefits
Cost Efficiency: Pay-as-you-go model reduces capital expenditure.
Scalability: Easily scale resources up or down based on demand.
Flexibility and Accessibility: Access services and data from anywhere with
an internet connection.
Innovation and Speed: Rapid deployment and innovation through cloud
services.

Flash Card #6
Resource Groups:
Logical containers to organize and manage related Azure resources.
Simplify access control and billing for resources within a group.
Can be nested for complex organizational structures.

Flash Card #7
Azure Regions:
East US
West Europe
Southeast Asia

Flash Card #8
Azure Services:
Azure Virtual Machines (VMs)
Azure Blob Storage
Azure App Service
Azure Networking Service
Azure Security Service
Azure Database Service.

Flash Card #9
Azure Pricing Models:
Pay-as-you-go
Reserved Instances
Spot Instances

Flash Card #10
Azure Identity and Access Management:
A cloud-based identity and access management service by Microsoft. It allows users to sign in and access resources.
Role-based access control (RBAC)
Centralized identity management for all users and applications.
Secure access control with multi-factor authentication (MFA).
Simplified application access with single sign-on (SSO).
Improved compliance and auditability.

Flash Card #11
Azure Virtual Networks:
Subnets
Virtual Network Peering
Network Security Groups (NSGs)

Flash Card #12
Azure Storage:
A scalable object storage solution for the cloud. It is used to store and manage unstructured data, such as documents, images, and videos.
Azure Storage Types:
- Blob Storage
- Table Storage
- File Storage

Flash Card #13
Azure Functions:
Serverless computing
Trigger types (HTTP, Timer, Queue)

Flash Card #14
Microsoft Defender for Cloud:
Threat detection
Security policies

Flash Card #15
Azure Governance:
Azure Policy
Azure Blueprints

Flash Card #16
Azure Backup and Disaster Recovery:
Azure Backup
Azure Site Recovery

Flash Card #17
Ways to Monitor the Health and Performance:
Azure Monitor: Provides comprehensive monitoring and analytics for resource performance, availability, and security.
Service Health: Offers insights into the overall health and status of Azure services.

Flash Card #18
Virtual Machine:
Virtual machines are scalable computing resources that run applications. They can be Windows or Linux-based and come in various sizes to meet different performance requirements.

Flash Card #19
Different VM Sizes:

Basic
Standard
Memory Optimized
Storage Optimized
High-Performance Computing.

Flash Card #20
Azure Storage Types:

Blobs (unstructured data)
Files (shared file systems)
Disks (block storage for VMs)
Queues (messaging)
Tables (NoSQL data store).

Flash Card #21
Azure App Service

A platform-as-a-service (PaaS) offering that enables building, hosting, and scaling web apps. It supports multiple programming languages and frameworks.

Azure Backup and Disaster Recovery

Flash Card #22
Azure Backup:

Definition: Azure Backup is a cloud-based service that provides data protection solutions for Azure virtual machines (VMs) and on-premises servers.

Retention Policy: Determines how long backup data is retained. Can be configured based on specific requirements.

Flash Card #23
Azure Site Recovery (ASR):

Purpose: Azure Site Recovery is used for disaster recovery and business continuity by replicating workloads from on-premises or other clouds to Azure.

Replication Types: ASR supports both asynchronous and synchronous replication.

Flash Card #24
Recovery Services Vault:

Definition: It is an Azure Resource Manager resource that stores backup data and Site Recovery orchestration details.

Configuration: A Recovery Services Vault must be created to configure and manage Azure Backup and Site Recovery.

Flash Card #25
Backup Policies:

Definition: Backup policies define the backup schedule, retention, and other settings for Azure Backup.

Example: Daily backups with a retention period of 30 days.

Flash Card #26
Instant File Recovery:
Capability: Azure Backup allows instant file recovery, enabling users to restore specific files without restoring the entire virtual machine.

Flash Card #27
Azure Backup Agent:
Usage: The Azure Backup agent is used for backing up files and folders on Windows servers and certain Linux distributions.

Flash Card #28
Azure Backup for Azure VMs:
Integration: Azure Backup seamlessly integrates with Azure Virtual Machines, providing a native backup solution.

Flash Card #29
Failover and Failback:

Failover: The process of transitioning from a primary site to a secondary site during a disaster.

Failback: The process of returning operations from the secondary site to the primary site after the primary site is restored.

Flash Card #30
Backup Alerts:
Importance: Configuring alerts ensures that administrators are notified of backup failures or other issues promptly.

Flash Card #31
Azure Backup for SQL Server:
Application Consistency: Azure Backup for SQL Server ensures application-consistent backups for databases.

Authentication

Flash Card #32

What is Authentication?

Authentication is the process of verifying the identity of a user, system, or entity.

Flash Card #33

Types of Authentication Factors:

1 **Something You Know:** Passwords, PINs
2. **Something You Have:** Smart cards, tokens
3. **Something You Are:** Biometrics (fingerprint, iris scan)

Flash Card #34

Multi-Factor Authentication (MFA):

MFA uses two or more authentication factors for enhanced security.

Flash Card #35

Token-Based Authentication:

Involves using a physical or virtual token (hardware or software) to authenticate users.

Flash Card #36

Biometric Authentication:

Uses unique physical or behavioral characteristics for identity verification.

Flash Card #37
Single Sign-On (SSO):

Allows users to access multiple systems or applications with a single set of credentials.

Authorization

Flash Card #38
What is Authorization?
Authorization is the process of granting or denying access rights to resources or services.

Flash Card #39
Access Control:
Determines what actions users or systems are allowed to perform on a resource.

Flash Card #40
Role-Based Access Control (RBAC):
Assigns permissions based on roles, simplifying management and ensuring least privilege

Flash Card #41
Permission Levels:

1 **Read:** Allows viewing but not modifying.
2. **Write:** Permits modification or creation of resources.
3. **Execute:** Grants the right to execute a program or script.

Flash Card #42
Access Control Lists (ACL):
Specifies permissions on individual resources, providing fine-grained control.

Flash Card #43
Policy-Based Authorization:
Defines access rules based on policies that govern resource usage.

Flash Card #44
Least Privilege Principle:
Users should have the minimum level of access necessary to perform their job functions

Flash Card #45
Session Management:
Ensures that access rights are maintained throughout a user's session and revoked when no longer needed.

Azure Cost Management

Flash Card #46
What is Azure Cost Management?
Azure Cost Management is a set of tools and services for managing and optimizing costs in Microsoft Azure.

Flash Card #47
Cost Tracking:
Helps monitor and analyze costs associated with Azure resources and services.

Flash Card #48
Budgets:
Allows setting spending limits to proactively manage and control costs.

Flash Card #49
Cost Alerts:
Sends notifications when actual costs exceed predefined thresholds.

Flash Card #50
Recommendations:
Provides suggestions for optimizing costs based on usage patterns.

Flash Card #51
Showback and Chargeback:

Enables organizations to allocate costs to different departments or projects for accountability.

Azure Pricing

Flash Card #52
Pay-as-You-Go:
Users pay for consumed resources on an hourly or per-minute basis, with no upfront commitment.

Flash Card #53
Reserved Instances:
Offers significant cost savings by committing to a one- or three-year term for specific virtual machine types.

Flash Card #54
Spot Instances:
Provides access to unused Azure compute capacity at a lower price, with the caveat that instances can be preempted.

Flash Card #55
Azure Hybrid Benefit:
Allows customers with Windows Server or SQL Server licenses to use them in Azure, reducing costs.

Flash Card #56
Azure Cost Estimator:

A tool to estimate costs before deploying resources, helping in budget planning.

Flash Card #57
Free Tier:

Offers a limited amount of Azure services at no cost, allowing users to explore and learn about Azure without incurring charges.

Flash Card #58
Azure Pricing Calculator:

A tool for estimating costs based on resource configurations and usage patterns.

Flash Card #59
Enterprise Agreements:

Customized agreements for large organizations, providing flexibility and cost savings.

Azure AI Services

Flash Card #60

What is Azure Cognitive Services

A suite of pre-built AI APIs for tasks like language understanding, computer vision, speech recognition, and text analysis.

Flash Card #61

What is Azure Machine Learning Service?

A platform for building, managing, and deploying machine learning models in the cloud.

Flash Card #62

What is Azure Databricks?

A cloud-based analytics service for large-scale data processing and machine learning with Apache Spark.

Flash Card #63

What is Azure Bot Service?

A platform for building intelligent chatbots and conversational AI applications

Flash Card #64
What is Azure Form Recognizer?

An AI service that automatically extracts and analyzes data from forms and documents

Flash Card #65
What is Azure Spatial Mapping?

A service that creates 3D spatial maps of indoor environments for applications like robotics and navigation.

Flash Card #66
What is Azure Custom Vision?

A service for building custom image recognition models without needing machine learning expertise.

Flash Card #67
What is Azure Anomaly Detector?

An AI service that detects unusual patterns in data for anomaly detection and fraud prevention.

Flash Card #68
What is Azure Text Analytics?

An AI service for analyzing text sentiment, keywords, and language features.

Flash Card #69

What is Azure Speech Services?

A suite of services for speech recognition, text-to-speech, and speech translation.

Flash Card #70

What are the benefits of using Azure AI services?

Faster development, reduced costs, scalability, access to pre-built AI capabilities, and integration with other Azure services.

Azure Database

Flash Card #71
Azure SQL Database:
Description: Fully managed relational database service in Azure.
Features:

- Automatic backups and patches.
- Built-in high availability and security.
- Scalability with various performance tiers.

Flash Card #72
Azure Cosmos DB
Description: Globally distributed, multi-model database service.
Features:

- Supports multiple data models (document, key-value, graph, column-family).
- Offers automatic and instant scalability.

Flash Card #73
Azure Database for MySQL
Description: Fully managed MySQL database service in Azure.
Features:

- Automated backups and security.
- Compatible with MySQL community edition.

Flash Card #74
Azure Database for PostgreSQL:
Description: Fully managed PostgreSQL database service in Azure.
Features:
- Built-in high availability and scaling options.
- Supports popular PostgreSQL extensions.

Flash Card #75
Azure Database for MariaDB
Description: Fully managed MariaDB database service in Azure.
Features:
- High availability and security features.
- Compatible with MariaDB community edition.

Flash Card #76
Azure Cache for Redis:
Description: In-memory data store service.
Features:
- Provides high-performance caching for applications.
- Supports data replication for high availability.

Flash Card #77
Azure Synapse Analytics (formerly SQL Data Warehouse):
Description: Analytical data warehouse service for large-scale data processing.
Features:

- Massively parallel processing (MPP) architecture.
- Integration with Power BI for visualization.

Flash Card #78
Azure Table Storage:
Description: NoSQL key-value store service.
Features:
- Designed for semi-structured data.
- Scalable and cost-effective storage solution.

Flash Card #79
Azure Database Migration Service:
Description: Service for migrating databases to Azure.
Features:
- Supports various source databases (SQL Server, MySQL, PostgreSQL).
- Minimizes downtime during migrations.

Flash Card #80
Azure Database for Cassandra:
Description: Managed Apache Cassandra service in Azure.
Features:
- Offers built-in high availability.
- Enables seamless scaling of Cassandra clusters.

Azure Support

Flash Card #81
What are the different tiers of Azure Support plans?
Basic, Standard, and Premium. Each tier offers different levels of support response times, service credits, and technical account manager access..

Flash Card #82
What is included in the Basic Support plan?
24/7 self-help support, access to Azure documentation and community forums, and incident submissions with a standard response time.

Flash Card #83
What are the benefits of the Standard Support plan?
Faster response times for incidents (4 hours or less), technical account manager access, and service credits for downtime

Flash Card #84
What does the Premium Support plan offer?
The fastest response times (1 hour or less), dedicated technical account manager, proactive monitoring and problem resolution, and service credits for downtime.

Flash Card#85
How can you submit a support ticket in Azure?
Through the Azure portal, by phone, or online chat.

Flash Card #86
What information should you include in my support ticket?
A clear description of the issue, subscription ID, resource details, and any error messages.

Flash Card #87
What are Azure Service Health notifications?
Proactive alerts about potential issues with Azure services, allowing you to prepare or take action.

Flash Card #88
What is Azure Advisor?
A free service that provides personalized recommendations for optimizing your Azure resources, security, and costs.

Flash Card #89
How can you get technical support for Azure Free Trial?
Limited support is available through online forums and documentation. Paid support plans are required for more comprehensive assistance.

Flash Card #90
What are some resources for self-help support in Azure?
Microsoft Learn modules, Azure documentation, Azure community forums, and the Azure blog.

Flash Card #91
What are the best practices for using Azure Support effectively?
Clearly describe your issue, provide relevant details, be proactive in monitoring your resources, and utilize self-help resources before escalating to paid support.

Azure Data and Analytics

Flash Card #92
What is Azure Synapse Analytics?
A cloud-based data warehouse for large-scale data analytics with enterprise-grade performance and security.

Flash Card #93
What are the benefits of using Azure Synapse Analytics?
Scalability, high performance, serverless architecture, built-in security, and integration with other Azure services.

Flash Card #94
What is Azure Data Lake Storage Gen2?
A highly scalable and secure object storage for storing large amounts of unstructured and semi-structured data.

Flash Card #95
What are the different tiers of Azure Data Lake Storage Gen2?
Hot, Cool, and Archive, offering different access speeds and costs.

Flash Card #96
What is Azure Data Explorer (Kusto)?
A fast and scalable analytics platform for exploring and analyzing large datasets in near real-time.

Flash Card #97
What are the advantages of using Azure Data Explorer?
Fast query performance, built-in data visualization, and support for various data sources.

Flash Card #98
What is Azure Databricks?
A managed Apache Spark service for large-scale data processing and machine learning.

Flash Card #99
What are the key features of Azure Databricks?
Unified workspace for data engineering, data science, and machine learning, integration with Azure data tools, and scalable clusters.

Flash Card #100
What is Azure Data Factory?
A cloud-based service for creating, orchestrating, and managing data pipelines.

Flash Card #101
What are the benefits of using Azure Data Factory?
Visual interface for building data pipelines, drag-and-drop connectors to various data sources, and automated data flow management.

Flash Card #102
What is Azure Power BI?
A cloud-based business intelligence platform for data visualization and analytics.

Flash Card #103
What are the key features of Azure Power BI?
Self-service data analysis, interactive dashboards and reports, and integration with various data sources

Flash Card # 104

How can you choose the right Azure Data and Analytics service for my needs?

Consider factors like data volume, query complexity, performance requirements, budget, and integration needs

Azure Networking Services

Flash Card # 105
What is Azure Virtual Network (VNet)?
A logically isolated network in the cloud, providing private IP addresses for your Azure resources

Flash Card # 106
What are subnets within a VNet?
Subdivisions of a VNet, defining specific IP address ranges for different groups of resources

Flash Card # 107
What are the two types of IP addresses in Azure?
Public IP addresses for internet access and private IP addresses for internal communication within the VNet

Flash Card # 108
What is a Network Security Group (NSG)?
A firewall that controls inbound and outbound network traffic to your resources

Flash Card # 109
What are the different ways to connect resources to a VNet?

Virtual machine network interfaces, Azure App Service, Cloud Services, and on-premises networks through VPN gateways.

Flash Card # 110
What is ExpressRoute?

A dedicated private connection between your on-premises network and Azure for increased performance and security

Flash Card # 111
What are Azure Load Balancers?

Distribute network traffic across multiple resources for high availability and scalability.

Flash Card # 112
What are Azure Application Gateways?

Layer 7 load balancers with additional features like web application firewall and routing based on URL paths.

Flash Card # 113
What is Azure Traffic Manager?

Routes user traffic based on performance, geographic location, or other criteria

Flash Card # 114
What is Azure VPN Gateway?

Creates secure tunnels for connecting your on-premises network to Azure over the public internet

Flash Card # 115
What are the best practices for designing secure Azure networks?

Segment networks with subnets and NSGs, use strong passwords and access controls, monitor network activity, and regularly update security configurations.

Azure Security Services

Flash Card # 116
Microsoft Entra ID
Description: Cloud-based identity and access management service.
Features:
- Single Sign-On (SSO) for applications.
- Multi-Factor Authentication (MFA) for enhanced security.

Flash Card # 117
Azure Sentinel:

Description: Cloud-native Security Information and Event Management (SIEM) service.

Features:

- Aggregates and analyzes security data across the organization.
- Uses machine learning for threat detection.

Flash Card # 118
Azure Security Center
Description: Centralized security management and advanced threat protection service.
Features:
- Security policy management and assessment.
- Continuous monitoring and threat detection.

Flash Card # 119
Azure Key Vault

Description: Securely manage and store sensitive information such as keys and secrets.

Features:

- Centralized key management.
- Integrates with Azure services and custom applications.

Flash Card # 120
Azure Information Protection

Description: Classify and protect sensitive data based on policies.

Features:

- Labeling and encryption of documents.
- Integration with Microsoft 365 applications

Flash Card # 121
Azure Firewall
Description: Managed network security service to protect Azure Virtual Network resources.
Features:
- Stateful firewall with high availability.
- Application and network-level filtering.

Flash Card # 122
Azure DDoS Protection

Description: Defends against Distributed Denial of Service (DDoS) attacks.

Features:

- Automatically mitigates DDoS attacks.
- Provides real-time attack analytics.

Flash Card # 123
Azure Advanced Threat Protection (ATP):

Description: Detects and investigates advanced attacks on-premises and in the cloud.

Features:

- Identifies malicious activities using behavioral analytics.
- Integration with Windows Defender ATP.

Flash Card # 124
Azure Bastion

Description: Secure and seamless RDP and SSH access to virtual machines.

Features:

- Eliminates the need for public IP addresses.
- Centralized and secure access management.

Flash Card # 125
Azure VPN Gateway

Description: Securely connect on-premises networks to Azure.

Features:

- Site-to-Site and Point-to-Site VPN connectivity.
- Supports various VPN protocols.

Azure Compute Services

Flash Card # 126
What is Azure Virtual Machines (VMs)?

On-demand, scalable virtualized servers in the cloud for deploying and managing Windows and Linux applications

Flash Card # 127
What are the different VM deployment options?

Pay-as-you-go, reserved instances, spot instances.

Flash Card # 128
What are the different VM sizes available?

Basic, Standard, Memory Optimized, Storage Optimized, High-Performance Computing.

Flash Card # 129
What is Azure Container Instances (ACIs)?

Serverless platform for running containerized applications without managing underlying infrastructure

Flash Card # 130
What are the benefits of using ACIs?

No infrastructure management, fast scaling, pay-per-second billing

Flash Card # 131
What is Azure App Service?

Platform for building, deploying, and scaling web apps, mobile apps, and APIs without managing servers

Flash Card # 132
What are the different pricing models for App Service?

Consumption plan, App Service plan, Free plan

Flash Card # 133
What are the deployment options for App Service?

Continuous deployment, manual deployment, deployment slots

Flash Card # 134
What is Azure Functions?

Serverless platform for running small pieces of code triggered by events.

Flash Card # 135
What are the benefits of using Azure Functions?

Serverless execution, pay-per-execution billing, triggers for various events

Flash Card # 136
What is Azure Kubernetes Service (AKS)?

Managed Kubernetes platform for deploying and managing containerized applications at scale

Flash Card # 137
What are the benefits of using AKS?

Simplified Kubernetes management, built-in security and monitoring, integration with other Azure services

Flash Card # 138

Which Azure compute service is the best choice for my needs?

Consider factors like application type, resource requirements, scalability needs, and budget.

Flash Card # 139

What are some considerations when designing a VNet?

Address space size: Choose enough addresses to accommodate future growth.

Subnet planning: Design subnets based on security needs and traffic flow.

NSG rules: Implement security policies for inbound and outbound traffic.

Route tables: Configure routes for efficient traffic flow within and outside the VNet

Azure Web Services

Flash Card # 140
Azure App Service?

Description: Fully managed platform for building, deploying, and scaling web apps.

Features:

- Supports multiple programming languages and frameworks.
- Integrated deployment slots for staging and testing.

Flash Card # 141
Azure Kubernetes Service (AKS):

Description: Managed Kubernetes container orchestration service.

Features:

- Simplifies deployment, management, and scaling of containerized applications.
- Supports automatic scaling based on demand.

Flash Card # 142
Azure Subscription Management:

Role-Based Access Control (RBAC):

- Manages access to Azure resources based on roles.
- Assigns permissions to users or groups.

Azure Policy:

- Enforces organizational standards and compliance.
- Automates policy enforcement across resources.

Azure Cost Management:

- Tools for monitoring, analyzing, and optimizing costs.
- Budgets, cost alerts, and recommendations are part of this service.

Flash Card # 143
Azure Logic Apps

Description: Service for automating workflows and integrating services, apps, and data.

Features:

- Visual design of workflows.
- Connects to a wide range of services and APIs.

Azure Mobile Services

Flash Card # 144
Azure Mobile Apps:

Description: Platform for building mobile apps that scale to millions of users.

Features:

- Supports offline data synchronization.
- Authentication and authorization capabilities.

Flash Card # 145
Azure Notification Hubs

Description: Service for sending push notifications to mobile devices.

Features:

- Cross-platform support (iOS, Android, Windows).
- Tag-based targeting for personalized notifications.

Flash Card # 146
Azure Mobile Engagement:

Description: Analytics and user engagement platform for mobile apps.

Features:

- In-app messaging and push notifications.
- Usage analytics for understanding user behavior.

Flash Card # 147
Azure DevOps for Mobile:

Description: Comprehensive set of development tools for building and deploying mobile apps.

Features:
- Version control, build automation, and release management.
- Continuous Integration and Continuous Deployment (CI/CD) pipelines.

Flash Card # 148
Azure Mobile Authenticator:

Description: Service for adding two-factor authentication to mobile apps.

Features:
- Enhances security with multi-factor authentication.
- Integration with Azure Active Directory.

Flash Card # 149
Azure AI Services for Mobile:

Description: APIs for adding AI capabilities to mobile apps.

Features:
- Vision, speech, language, and search APIs for enhanced functionality.
- Enables developers to build intelligent mobile applications.

Azure Storage

Flash Card # 150
Azure Storage Account:

Definition: A storage account in Azure provides a unique namespace to store and access data objects in the cloud.

Features:

- Supports multiple types of storage services (Blob, File, Queue, Table).
- Enables secure and scalable data storage.

Flash Card # 151
Azure Blob Storage:

Description: Object storage service for large amounts of unstructured data.

Features:

- Supports various data types, including text, binary, and images.
- Scalable and durable storage solution.

Flash Card # 152
Azure File Storage:

Description: Fully managed file share in the cloud.

Features:

- Enables sharing files across multiple virtual machines.
- Supports the Server Message Block (SMB) protocol.

Flash Card # 153
Azure Queue Storage:

Description: Scalable message queue service for decoupling components of cloud applications.

Features:

- Supports asynchronous communication between application components.
- Enables building resilient and loosely coupled applications.

Flash Card # 154
Azure Table Storage:

Description: NoSQL data store for semi-structured data.

Features:

- Schema-less storage allows flexibility in data structure.
- Suitable for storing large amounts of data with minimal latency

Flash Card # 155
Azure Policy Assignment:

Definition:

- Assigning policies to a specific scope, such as a subscription or resource group.
- Governs the behavior of resources within that scope.

Use Cases:

- Enforcing specific compliance standards.
- Implementing naming conventions or resource tagging requirements.

Flash Card # 156
Azure Disk Storage:

Description: Persistent, high-performance block storage for virtual machines.

Features:

- Supports both Standard and Premium storage tiers.
- Can be used as an OS disk or data disk for virtual machines.

Flash Card # 157
Azure Storage Explorer:

Description: A graphical interface for managing Azure Storage accounts.

Features:

- Browse and manage Blob, File, Table, and Queue services.
- Supports data transfer and manipulation.

Flash Card # 158
Azure Data Lake Storage:

Description: Scalable and secure data lake solution for big data analytics.

Features:

- Integrates with analytics services like Azure Databricks and Azure Synapse Analytics.
- Hierarchical namespace for efficient data organization.

Flash Card # 159
Azure Storage Replication:

Options:

- **Locally Redundant Storage (LRS):** Copies data within the same region.
- **Geo-Redundant Storage (GRS):** Replicates data to a secondary region for data durability.
- **Read-Access Geo-Redundant Storage (RA-GRS):** Provides read access to the secondary region

Flash Card # 160
Azure Storage Security:

- Uses Shared Access Signatures (SAS) for granting limited access to resources.
- Integrates with Azure Active Directory for identity-based access control.

Azure Monitoring and Management

Flash Card # 161

Azure Monitor: Access Control

Definition: Azure Monitor is a comprehensive solution for collecting, analyzing, and acting on telemetry from Azure resources.

Features:

- Provides insights into the performance and health of applications and resources.
- Integrates with other Azure monitoring services.

Flash Card # 162

Azure Log Analytics:

Description: A service within Azure Monitor that collects and analyzes log and telemetry data from Azure resources.

Features:

- Supports custom queries for log data.
- Enables advanced analytics and visualization.

Flash Card # 163

Azure Application Insights:

Description: An Application Performance Management (APM) service for monitoring live applications.

Features:

- Detects and diagnoses issues in web applications.
- Provides real-time insights into application performance.

Flash Card # 164
Azure Security Center:
Description: A unified security management system that strengthens the security posture across all Azure resources.
Features:
- Continuous security assessment and threat detection.
- Integration with Azure Policy for compliance management.

Flash Card # 165
Azure Policy:
Definition: Azure Policy is a service that helps you create, assign, and manage policies to enforce compliance within your Azure environment.
Features:
- Define and enforce policies for resources.
- Assess and remediate non-compliance.

Flash Card # 166
Azure Resource Manager (ARM):
Description: A management layer in Azure that enables resource deployment and management in a declarative manner.
Features:
- Defines resources using JSON templates.
- Provides consistent management across resources.

Flash Card # 167

Azure Automation:

Description: A cloud-based automation service for orchestrating tasks and workflows across Azure and non-Azure environments.

Features:

- Runbooks for automating common tasks.
- Desired State Configuration for maintaining consistent configurations.

Flash Card # 168

Azure Policy Insights:

Description: A feature within Azure Policy that provides detailed insights into policy compliance across resources.

Features:

- View compliance at scale.
- Drill down into non-compliant resources for remediation.

Flash Card # 169

Azure Advisor:

Definition: Azure Advisor is a service that provides recommendations on best practices for optimizing Azure resources.

Features:

- Analyzes resource configurations and usage.
- Offers actionable recommendations for improving performance, security, and cost

83

Flash Card # 170

Azure Governance:

Definition: The set of practices and policies for managing resources and enforcing compliance in the cloud.

Components:

- Azure Policy, Blueprints, Management Groups.
- Hierarchies for organization and management.

Azure Internet of Things (IoT)

Flash Card # 171
Azure IoT Hub:
Definition: A fully managed service for bi-directional communication between IoT applications and devices.
Components:
- Securely connect and manage IoT devices at scale.
- Supports protocols like MQTT, AMQP, and HTTP.

Flash Card # 172
Azure IoT Central:
Definition: A fully managed IoT software-as-a-service (SaaS) solution for building and scaling IoT applications.
Components:
- Simplifies IoT application development with pre-built templates.
- Offers device connectivity and management

Flash Card # 173
Azure IoT Edge:
Definition: Extends IoT functionality to the edge devices, enabling processing closer to the data source.
Components:
- Deploy and run Azure services on edge devices.
- Enables offline operation and reduced latency.

Flash Card # 174
Azure IoT Solutions Accelerators:
Description: Pre-built, customizable solutions for common IoT scenarios.
Examples:

- **Remote Monitoring:** Monitors and manages devices remotely.
- **Predictive Maintenance:** Identifies potential equipment issues.

Flash Card # 175
Azure Digital Twins:
Definition: A service for creating comprehensive digital models of physical environments and assets.
Components:

- Enables simulation and analysis of real-world scenarios.
- Integrates with Azure IoT solutions.

Flash Card # 176
Azure Sphere:
Definition: A secured, connected microcontroller unit (MCU) platform for building IoT devices.
Components:

- Combines hardware, OS, and cloud services for enhanced security.
- Enables over-the-air updates and maintenance.

Flash Card # 177
Azure IoT SDKs:
Definition: Software development kits for various programming languages to build IoT applications
Components:
- Azure IoT SDK for C, Python, Node.js, Java, etc.
- Simplifies device and service communication.

Flash Card # 178
Azure Stream Analytics for IoT:
Definition: Real-time analytics service for processing streaming data from IoT devices.
Components:
- Ingests, processes, and analyzes data in real-time.
- Integrates with other Azure services.

Flash Card # 179
Azure IoT Security:
Components:
- **Device Identity:** Securely authenticate and authorize devices.
- **Device Twin:** Store and retrieve device-specific metadata.
- **Device Provisioning Service (DPS):** Automate device provisioning at scale.

Flash Card # 180

Azure IoT Reference Architectures:

Definition: Proven design patterns for implementing IoT solutions on Azure.

Examples:

- **Connected Factory:** Illustrates IoT implementation in manufacturing.
- **Smart City:** Demonstrates IoT deployment for urban environments.

How to Interact with Azure

Flash Card # 181

Azure Portal:

Definition: Web-based management interface for Azure services.

Components:

- Graphical user interface for resource management.
- Access to various Azure services and configurations.

Flash Card # 182

Azure CLI (Command-Line Interface):

Definition: Cross-platform command-line tool for managing Azure resources.

Components:

- Scriptable and supports automation.
- Available for Windows, macOS, and Linux.

Flash Card # 183

Azure PowerShell:

Definition: PowerShell module for managing Azure resources.

Components:

- Leverages PowerShell scripting capabilities.
- Integrates with Azure Resource Manager.

Flash Card # 184

Azure REST API:

Definition: Representational State Transfer (REST) API for programmatically interacting with Azure

Components:

- Allows developers to build custom solutions and automate tasks.
- Supports CRUD operations for Azure resources.

Flash Card # 185

Azure SDKs (Software Development Kits):

Definition: Libraries and packages for various programming languages to interact with Azure services.

Components:

- Available for languages like C#, Python, Java, Node.js, etc.
- Simplifies integration with Azure services in application code.

Flash Card # 186

Azure Resource Manager (ARM) Templates:

Definition: Declarative JSON templates for deploying and managing Azure resources.

Components:

- Infrastructure as Code (IaC) approach.
- Enables consistent and repeatable deployments.

Flash Card # 187

Azure DevOps:

Definition: A set of development tools for automating the deployment and management of Azure resources.

Components:

- Continuous Integration and Continuous Deployment (CI/CD) pipelines.

- Source code management, build, release, and test capabilities.

Flash Card # 188

Azure PowerShell DSC (Desired State Configuration):

Definition: PowerShell extension for configuring and managing Azure resources in a declarative manner.

Components:
- Defines the desired state of resources.
- Ensures consistency and compliance.

Flash Card # 189

Azure Mobile App:

Definition: Mobile application for monitoring and managing Azure resources on the go.

Components:
- View resource health, alerts, and metrics.
- Execute basic management tasks from a mobile device..

Flash Card # 190

Azure Cloud Shell:

Definition: Browser-based shell provided by Azure for managing resources.

Components:
- Supports Azure CLI, PowerShell, and various development tools.
- Accessible from the Azure Portal

Azure Marketplace

Flash Card # 191
Azure Marketplace:

Definition: An online store for discovering, trying, and purchasing applications and services certified to run on Azure.

Components:

- Offers a wide range of solutions from third-party vendors.
- Simplifies the deployment of applications on Azure.

Flash Card # 192
Solutions in Azure Marketplace:

Types:

- **Virtual Machine Images:** Pre-configured virtual machine images for quick deployment.
- **SaaS Applications:** Software as a Service solutions accessible over the internet.
- **Data Services:** Databases, storage, and analytics services.

Flash Card # 193
Benefits for Customers:

Ease of Deployment: Quickly deploy and configure solutions without extensive setup.

Certification: Solutions are certified to run on Azure, ensuring compatibility and performance.

Billing Integration: Charges for Marketplace solutions can be integrated with Azure billing.

Flash Card # 194
Benefits for Publishers:

Global Reach: Reach a global audience of Azure customers.

Monetization: Monetize applications and services through the Marketplace.

Simplified Distribution: Use Azure Marketplace as a distribution channel.

Flash Card # 195
Cloud Characteristics:

On-Demand Self-Service:

- Users can provision and manage resources as needed without human intervention.

Broad Network Access:

- Services are accessible over the network and can be accessed through various devices.

Resource Pooling:

- Computing resources are pooled to serve multiple customers, with different physical and virtual resources dynamically assigned and reassigned.

Rapid Elasticity:

- Resources can be rapidly scaled up or down to handle demand.

Measured Service:

- Cloud resources are metered, and users are billed based on their usage.

Flash Card # 196
Azure Marketplace Categories:

- **Compute:** Virtual machine images, container solutions.
- **Networking:** Network appliances, security solutions.
- **Storage:** Data storage and backup solutions.
- **Web:** Web applications, content management systems.
- **Databases:** Database management systems, data warehousing.

Flash Card # 197
Private Offers:

Definition: Customized agreements between publishers and customers for private procurement.

Features:

- Tailored pricing and terms based on customer needs.
- Allows negotiation and custom licensing.

Flash Card # 198
Azure Marketplace Security:

Certification Process: Solutions undergo a certification process for security and compliance.

Azure Active Directory Integration: Supports integration with Azure AD for identity management.

Azure Policy: Enforces security policies on deployed Marketplace solutions.

Flash Card # 199
Azure Kubernetes Service (AKS) Marketplace:

Description: A section of Azure Marketplace specifically for Kubernetes applications.

Features:

- Simplifies deployment of containerized applications on AKS.
- Offers a variety of Helm charts and Kubernetes applications.

Flash Card # 200
Azure Virtual Machine Offers:

Variety of Operating Systems: Windows, Linux, and specialized OS images.

Pre-configured Software: VMs with pre-installed applications for specific use cases.

Different Sizes and Performance Tiers: Choose VM sizes based on workload requirements.

Flash Card # 201
Azure Marketplace for Azure Government:

Description: A version of Azure Marketplace designed for Azure Government customers.

Features:

- Solutions certified for use in Azure Government environments.
- Ensures compliance with government regulations and standards.

Azure Physical Infrastructure

Flash Card # 202
Azure Regions:

Definition: A geographical area containing one or more data centers with Azure resources.

Features:

- Each region is isolated and has its own power, cooling, and networking infrastructure.
- Enables redundancy and availability across multiple locations.

Flash Card # 203
Azure Availability Zones:

Description: Unique physical locations within an Azure region equipped with independent power, cooling, and networking.

Features:

- Provides high availability and fault tolerance.
- Applications can be distributed across multiple zones for resilience.

Flash Card # 204
Azure Data Centers:

Definition: Facilities housing servers, storage, and networking equipment for running Azure services.

Features:

- Redundant power and cooling systems.
- Physical security measures to protect infrastructure.

Flash Card # 205
Azure Datacenter Architecture:

Components:

- **Compute Nodes:** Physical servers for running virtual machines.
- **Storage Nodes:** Servers dedicated to storage infrastructure.
- **Network Devices:** Routers, switches, and load balancers.

Connectivity:

- High-speed, low-latency connections between components.
- Connectivity to the internet and Azure backbone network.

Flash Card # 206
Azure Backbone Network:

Definition: A high-speed, private network connecting all Azure regions globally.

Purpose:

- Enables fast and reliable communication between Azure data centers.
- Facilitates data replication and redundancy.

Flash Card # 207
Azure Edge Locations:

Description: Smaller data centers strategically located to bring Azure services closer to end-users.

Use Cases:

- Content Delivery Networks (CDN) for faster content delivery.

- Edge computing for low-latency applications.

Flash Card # 208
Azure ExpressRoute:

Definition: A dedicated private connection between on-premises data centers and Azure.

Features:

- Offers more reliability and lower latency than public internet connections.
- Enables a private and dedicated network connection.

Flash Card # 209
Azure Scale Units:

Definition: The basic building blocks of Azure data centers, consisting of compute, storage, and network resources.

Purpose:

- Facilitates modular and scalable expansion of Azure infrastructure.
- Allows efficient resource allocation and management.

Flash Card # 210
Azure Security Measures:

Physical Security:

- Restricted access to data centers with biometric authentication.
- Surveillance cameras and security personnel.

Logical Security:

- Encryption of data in transit and at rest.
- Network security measures, including firewalls and DDoS protection.

Flash Card # 211
Azure Immersive Datacenter Experience (ADX):

Description: A virtual tour providing insights into Azure data centers.

Features:

- Interactive exploration of data center infrastructure.
- Educational resource for understanding Azure's physical presence.

Azure Management Infrastructure

Flash Card # 212
What is Azure Resource Manager (ARM)?
A unified platform for managing and deploying Azure resources through templates and APIs

Flash Card # 213
What are the benefits of using ARM?
Consistent resource management, automated deployments, infrastructure as code, and role-based access control.

Flash Card # 214
What are Azure Resource Groups?
Logical containers for organizing and managing related Azure resources.

Flash Card # 215
What are the benefits of using Resource Groups?
Simplified billing, access control, and deployment for groups of resources.

Flash Card # 216
What is Azure Monitor?
A comprehensive service for monitoring performance, health, and availability of Azure resources

Flash Card # 217

What are the key features of Azure Monitor?

Metrics, logs, alerts, application insights, and proactive problem detection.

Flash Card # 218

What is Azure Policy?

Allows defining and enforcing policies to govern resource creation and configuration for compliance and security.

Flash Card # 219

What are the benefits of using Azure Policy?

Enforces consistent standards, simplifies governance, and reduces compliance risks.

Flash Card # 220

What is Azure Blueprints?

A service for defining and deploying standardized environments with infrastructure, security, and governance configurations.

Flash Card # 221

What are the benefits of using Azure Blueprints?

Repeatable deployments, consistent environments, and accelerated cloud adoption.

Flash Card # 222
What is Azure Cost Management?

Provides tools for monitoring, analyzing, and optimizing Azure resource costs

Flash Card # 223
What are the benefits of using Azure Cost Management?

Identifies cost savings opportunities, budgets resource spending, and optimizes resource utilization.

Flash Card # 224
What are the best practices for managing Azure infrastructure effectively?

Utilize ARM templates, organize resources with groups, monitor performance with Azure Monitor, define policies for governance, leverage Blueprints for standardized environments, and track costs with Cost Management.

Flash Card # 225
What are some different types of VNets?

Hub-spoke: Central VNet connects to multiple spoke VNets for a hierarchical structure.

Peering: Connect VNets directly for efficient resource communication.

ExpressRoute: Connect your VNet to your on-premises network for hybrid deployments.

Azure Container Instances (ACI)

Flash Card # 226
What is Azure Container Instances (ACI)?

A serverless platform for running containerized applications without managing underlying infrastructure.

Flash Card # 227
What are the benefits of using ACI?

No infrastructure management: Pay-per-second billing eliminates server provisioning and maintenance.

Fast scaling: Quickly scale containers up or down based on demand.

Simple deployment: Deploy container images directly from registries like Azure Container Registry or Docker Hub.

Integration with other Azure services: Works seamlessly with other Azure services like Azure Storage and Azure Functions.

Flash Card # 228
What are the limitations of ACI?

Limited resource availability: Resources are shared with other users, potentially impacting performance.

No persistent storage: Containers cannot access persistent storage by default.

No custom networking: Limited network configuration options compared to Azure Kubernetes Service (AKS).

Flash Card # 229
What are the different deployment options for ACI?

Azure portal: Manually deploy containers through the Azure portal.

CLI: Use the Azure CLI commands to automate deployments.

APIs: Integrate ACI with your CI/CD pipeline using the REST API.

Flash Card # 230
When should you use ACI instead of Azure Kubernetes Service (AKS)?

For simple, short-lived containerized tasks.

When managing infrastructure is not desired.

For cost-sensitive applications with variable workloads

Flash Card # 231
When should you use AKS instead of ACI?

For complex containerized applications requiring custom networking and persistent storage.

For applications requiring high availability and scalability.

When managing and controlling the container orchestration is necessary.

Azure Core Solutions and Management Tools

Flash Card # 232
What are the key components of a VNet?
Address space: Defines the private IP address range for your resources.

Subnets: Divide the VNet into smaller address ranges for granular control.

Network Security Groups (NSGs): Define inbound and outbound security rules for resources.

Route tables: Control how traffic flows within and outside the VNet.

Flash Card # 233
What are the benefits of using Azure IoT Hub?

Scalability: Supports millions of devices with secure communication.

Device management: Remotely configure, deploy updates, and monitor devices.

Data ingestion and processing: Collect and analyze device telemetry data.

Rule engine: Define actions based on device events and data

Flash Card # 234
What are the benefits of using Azure IoT Central?
Pre-built dashboards and templates: Quick setup and visualization of device data.
Device management: Manage devices without writing code.
Rule builder: Create rules for device actions and alerts.
Scalability: Supports large numbers of devices..

Flash Card # 235
What types of Azure Load Balancer are available?

Application Load Balancer: Routes traffic based on application-layer attributes like URL paths or headers.

Basic Load Balancer: Routes traffic based on network-layer attributes like IP addresses or ports.

Flash Card # 236
What are the benefits of using Azure Sphere?

Enhanced security: Hardware-based security features protect devices from attacks.

Simplified development: Focus on application logic without low-level security concerns.

Cloud connectivity: Secure communication with Azure services.

Flash Card # 237
What are the key features of Azure Load Balancer?
Health probes: Monitor backend health and automatically remove unhealthy instances from the pool.
Traffic distribution: Distributes traffic based on chosen method (round robin, weighted, etc.).
Backend pools: Group backend resources for load balancing.
Load balancing rules: Define how traffic is routed to specific backend pools.

Flash Card # 238
What are the benefits of using Azure Digital Twins?

Improved operational efficiency: Monitor and optimize asset performance.

Predictive maintenance: Identify potential issues before they occur.

Enhanced decision-making: Gain insights from simulated scenarios.

Flash Card # 239
What is Azure Resource Manager (ARM)?
A unified platform for managing and deploying Azure resources using templates and APIs

Flash Card # 240
What are the benefits of using ARM?
Automated deployments: Deploy infrastructure consistently and efficiently.

Infrastructure as code: Manage infrastructure through code for version control and repeatability.

Role-based access control: Define granular access permissions for resources.

Flash Card # 241
What is Azure Monitor?
A comprehensive service for monitoring performance, health, and availability of Azure resources.

Flash Card # 242
What are the benefits of using Azure Monitor?

Metrics and logs: Collect and analyze resource data for troubleshooting and optimization.

Alerts: Set up notifications for critical events.

Application Insights: Monitor performance and diagnose issues in web applications.

Flash Card # 243
What is Azure Cost Management?

Provides tools for monitoring, analyzing, and optimizing Azure resource costs.

Flash Card # 244
What are the benefits of using Azure Cost Management?

Identify cost savings opportunities: Analyze resource usage and recommend optimizations.

Set budgets and track spending: Monitor costs against defined budgets.

Reserve resources for predictable savings: Secure discounted rates for frequently used resources.

Azure Zero Trust Model

Flash Card # 245
What is the core principle of the Azure Zero Trust Model?

Never trust, always verify. This means continuously authenticating and authorizing users, devices, applications, and resources before granting access, regardless of location or network position.

Flash Card # 246
What are the key pillars of the Azure Zero Trust Model?

Identity: Verify user identity with strong authentication and access control.

Devices: Ensure device health, compliance, and secure access before granting connectivity.

Applications: Implement least privilege access and continuous authorization for applications.

Data: Protect data at rest, in transit, and in use with encryption and access controls.

Networks: Segment networks and use micro-segmentation for granular access control.

Flash Card # 247
What are the benefits of using the Azure Zero Trust Model?

Enhanced security: Reduces the attack surface and minimizes the impact of breaches.

Improved compliance: Aligns with security best practices and regulations.

Increased agility: Enables secure access from anywhere, anytime.

Reduced costs: Optimizes resource utilization and minimizes risk of data breaches.

Flash Card # 248
What are some Azure services that support the Zero Trust Model?

Azure Active Directory (Azure AD) for identity management and access control.

Azure Defender for endpoint protection and device health monitoring.

Azure Sentinel for security information and event management (SIEM).

Azure Security Center for comprehensive security insights and threat detection.

Azure Network Security Groups (NSGs) and Azure Firewall for network segmentation and access control.

Flash Card # 249
What are some best practices for implementing the Azure Zero Trust Model?

Identify and prioritize critical assets and data.

Implement multi-factor authentication (MFA) for all users.

Patch and update devices regularly.

Grant least privilege access based on user roles and needs.

Monitor and audit user activity for suspicious behavior.

Continuously review and update security policies and procedures.

Azure Defense in Depth

Flash Card # 250
What is Azure Defense in Depth (DiD)?

A layered security approach that involves multiple security controls stacked on top of each other to create a more robust defense against cyber threats. No single point of failure exists, making it harder for attackers to gain access to your resources.

Flash Card # 251
What are the key layers of Azure Defense in Depth?
Physical Security: Securing physical data centers and equipment with access controls, surveillance, and environmental protections.
Identity & Access Management: Implementing strong authentication, authorization, and least privilege access controls for users and applications.
Network Security: Segmenting networks, using firewalls and intrusion detection/prevention systems (IDS/IPS), and encrypting network traffic.
Compute Security: Implementing security configurations for virtual machines, containers, and other compute resources, including patching and vulnerability management.

Flash Card # 252
What are the benefits of using Azure Defense in Depth?

Increased security: Multi-layered protection reduces the risk of successful attacks.

Improved compliance: Aligns with security best practices and regulations.

Enhanced resilience: Minimizes the impact of breaches and facilitates faster recovery.

Flexibility: Adapt the approach based on specific security needs and risks.

Flash Card # 253
What are some Azure services that support Azure Defense in Depth?

Azure Active Directory (Azure AD) for identity and access management.

Azure Security Center for threat detection and security insights.

Azure Sentinel for security information and event management (SIEM).

Azure Defender for endpoint protection, vulnerability management, and threat intelligence.

Azure Key Vault for managing and safeguarding encryption keys.

Azure Firewall and Network Security Groups (NSGs) for network segmentation and access control.

Azure Monitor for performance and security monitoring.

Flash Card # 254
What are some best practices for implementing Azure Defense in Depth?

Conduct regular security assessments and penetration testing.

Continuously update and patch systems and software.

Implement multi-factor authentication (MFA) for all users.

Encrypt sensitive data at rest and in transit.

Segment your network and implement granular access controls.

Monitor system activity for suspicious behavior.

Have a documented incident response plan and practice it regularly.

Flash Card # 255
What are the three main goals of securing network connectivity?

Confidentiality (ensuring data privacy), Integrity (ensuring data accuracy), and Availability (ensuring access to data/resources)

Flash Card # 256
What are some common threats to network security?

Malware, unauthorized access, data breaches, denial-of-service attacks, and man-in-the-middle attacks.

Flash Card # 257
What is Network Segmentation?

Dividing a network into smaller, isolated segments to limit the potential impact of security breaches

Flash Card # 258
What are Firewalls and how do they work?

Firewalls act as security barriers, filtering incoming and outgoing traffic based on defined rules.

Flash Card # 259
What are the different types of firewalls?

Packet filtering firewalls, stateful firewalls, application-level firewalls, and next-generation firewalls (NGFWs).

Flash Card # 260
What is encryption and how does it help secure network communication?

Encryption scrambles data, making it unreadable without the decryption key, ensuring confidentiality.

Flash Card # 261
What are some common encryption protocols used in network security?

AES, RSA, TLS/SSL, and SSH

Flash Card # 262
What is Virtual Private Network (VPN) and how does it work?

VPN creates a secure tunnel over a public network, encrypting communication between devices or networks

Flash Card # 263
What are some important network security best practices?

Regularly update software and firmware, implement strong passwords and access controls, monitor network activity for suspicious behavior, and conduct security audits

Flash Card # 264
What are some tools and technologies used for network security monitoring and analysis?

Security Information and Event Management (SIEM) systems, Intrusion Detection/Prevention Systems (IDS/IPS), and network traffic analysis tools.

Flash Card # 265
What are some cloud-based solutions for securing network connectivity?

Azure Security Center, Amazon GuardDuty, Google Cloud Armor, and Cloudflare

Distributed Denial-of-Service Attacks (DDoS)

Flash Card # 266
What is a Distributed Denial-of-Service (DDoS) attack?

An attempt to overwhelm a target system or network with a flood of traffic, making it unavailable to legitimate users

Flash Card # 267
What are the different types of DDoS attacks?

Volumetric attacks (flooding with traffic), application-layer attacks (targeting specific vulnerabilities), and protocol attacks (exploiting protocol flaws).

Flash Card # 268
What are common motivations for DDoS attacks?

Extortion, cyberwarfare, activism, and competition

Flash Card # 269
What are the main components of a DDoS attack botnet?

Command and control server, infected devices (zombies), and attack tools

Flash Card # 270

How can you mitigate DDoS attacks?

Implementing DDoS mitigation services, filtering traffic, using rate limiting, and leveraging redundant infrastructure

Flash Card # 271

What are some best practices for DDoS preparedness?

Develop a DDoS response plan, educate employees, regularly backup data, and test your defenses.

Flash Card # 272

What are some challenges in defending against DDoS attacks?

Evolving attack techniques, difficulty in distinguishing legitimate and malicious traffic, and large-scale attack volume

Flash Card # 273

What are the legal implications of launching a DDoS attack?

DDoS attacks are illegal in most countries and can result in significant penalties.

Flash Card # 274

What are some resources for learning more about DDoS attacks?

A unified cloud security platform offering comprehensive protection for your Azure, AWS, Google Cloud Platform (GCP), and hybrid environments

Azure Key Vault

Flash Card # 275
What is Azure Key Vault?

A managed service for securely storing and controlling access to secrets like passwords, API keys, certificates, and cryptographic keys.

Flash Card # 276
What are the benefits of using Key Vault?

Centralized security: Store secrets in a secure environment with access control and logging.

Enhanced protection: Secure secrets with hardware security modules (HSMs) for added security.

Simplified management: Manage secrets in one place with role-based access control (RBAC).

Improved compliance: Meet security and compliance requirements with audit trails and access control.

Integration with other Azure services: Integrates seamlessly with other Azure services like Azure App Service and Azure Functions.

Flash Card # 277
What are the different types of secrets you can store in Key Vault?

Secrets: Passwords, API keys, connection strings, etc.

Keys: RSA keys, ECC keys, and symmetric keys for encryption and decryption.

Certificates: SSL/TLS certificates and self-signed certificates

Flash Card # 278
How does Key Vault manage access to secrets?

Access policies: Define who can access specific secrets using Azure Active Directory (AD) identities or managed identities.

Azure RBAC: Control access at the vault and secret level for granular control.

Flash Card # 279
What are some security features of Key Vault?

HSM protection: Available for select key types for an extra layer of security.

Double Key Encryption (DKE): Keys are encrypted with both a master key and a customer-managed key for added security.

Regular security audits: Microsoft conducts regular security audits of Key Vault

Flash Card # 280
How can you access secrets stored in Key Vault?

Azure Portal: Access secrets through the Azure portal UI.

Azure CLI: Use Azure CLI commands to manage secrets.

SDKs: Use SDKs in various programming languages to access secrets programmatically

Flash Card # 281

What are some best practices for using Key Vault?

Use strong passwords and multi-factor authentication for access.

Grant least privilege access to secrets.

Rotate secrets regularly.

Monitor access logs and detect suspicious activity.

Use managed identities for improved security and convenience

Azure Information Protection (AIP)

Flash Card # 282
What is Azure Information Protection (AIP)?

A cloud-based solution for classifying, labeling, and protecting sensitive information across devices, apps, and cloud services

Flash Card # 283
What are the benefits of using AIP?

Data confidentiality: Ensures unauthorized access to sensitive information is prevented.

Data classification: Classifies data based on sensitivity levels for informed protection decisions.

Policy enforcement: Automatically applies protection based on defined policies.

Data encryption: Encrypts sensitive data at rest and in transit for added security.

Enhanced compliance: Helps meet data privacy and regulatory compliance requirements.

Flash Card # 284
What are the key components of AIP?

Labels: Tags applied to data to define its sensitivity level and protection settings.

Policies: Define how data is protected based on its label and user context.

Client agents: Installed on devices to enforce policies and control information access.

Azure Information Protection service: Cloud-based service that manages labels, policies, and reporting.

Flash Card # 285
How does AIP classify data?

Users can manually apply labels based on pre-defined sensitivity levels (e.g., Confidential, Internal, Public).

AIP can also automatically classify data based on keywords, content type, or other criteria.

Flash Card # 286
What types of protection can AIP enforce?

Encryption: Encrypts data at rest and in transit using industry-standard algorithms.

Visual markings: Applies visual indicators to documents and emails to signal sensitivity.

Access restrictions: Controls who can access data based on labels, user roles, and device compliance.

Information rights management (IRM): Restricts actions users can take on sensitive data (e.g., printing, forwarding).

Flash Card # 287
How does AIP integrate with other Microsoft services?

Works seamlessly with Microsoft 365, Azure Active Directory, and other cloud services.

Utilizes Azure Rights Management (Azure RMS) for advanced IRM capabilities.

Flash Card # 288
What are some best practices for using AIP?

Define clear data classification policies.

Educate users on labeling and data protection guidelines.

Monitor and audit access to sensitive data.

Regularly review and update your AIP policies and configurations.

Advanced Threat Protection (ATP)

Flash Card # 289
What is Advanced Threat Protection (ATP)?

A general term for security solutions that go beyond traditional antivirus and firewall protection to detect and respond to sophisticated cyber threats.

Flash Card # 290
What are some specific examples of ATP solutions?

Microsoft Defender for Endpoint (formerly Microsoft Defender Advanced Threat Protection)

- Azure Sentinel
- Crowdstrike Falcon
- Palo Alto Networks Cortex XDR
- McAfee Endpoint Security

Flash Card # 291
What are the key capabilities of ATP solutions?

Endpoint protection: Protects devices from malware, exploits, and other threats.

Threat detection and investigation: Uses advanced analytics and machine learning to identify suspicious activity.

Automated response: Takes actions to contain threats and mitigate damage.

Threat intelligence: Provides insights into the latest threats and vulnerabilities.

Security information and event management (SIEM): Aggregates and analyzes security data from multiple sources.

Flash Card # 292
What are the benefits of using ATP solutions?

Improved security posture: Provides deeper protection against advanced threats.

Reduced risk of breaches: Detects and responds to threats faster.

Improved compliance: Helps meet security and compliance requirements.

Enhanced visibility: Provides centralized visibility into security threats and incidents.

Streamlined security operations: Automates tasks and simplifies threat management.

Flash Card # 293
What are some of the challenges of using ATP solutions?

Cost: Advanced features may come with higher costs.

Complexity: Implementing and managing ATP solutions can be complex.

False positives: Can generate alerts for non-malicious activity.

Skilled personnel: Requires skilled personnel to interpret alerts and take action.

Flash Card # 294
How do you choose the right ATP solution for your needs?

Consider your security needs and budget.

Evaluate the features and capabilities of different solutions.

Read reviews and compare pricing.

Consult with security experts

Flash Card # 295
What are some best practices for using ATP solutions?

Keep your software up to date.

Educate your employees on cybersecurity awareness.

Regularly review and update your security policies.

Monitor your security logs and investigate suspicious activity.

Conduct regular security assessments and penetration testing

Azure Sentinel

Flash Card # 296
What is Azure Sentinel?

A cloud-native Security Information and Event Management (SIEM) solution for collecting, analyzing, and responding to security threats across your Azure, hybrid, and on-premises environments.

Flash Card # 297
What are the key capabilities of Azure Sentinel?

Data ingestion: Collects security data from various sources like Azure services, endpoints, Active Directory, and third-party tools.

Log analysis: Uses machine learning and analytics to detect suspicious activity and potential threats.

Threat hunting: Enables proactive threat hunting with built-in queries and custom KQL queries.

Incident management: Provides tools to investigate and respond to security incidents in a coordinated manner.

Automation: Supports automation of tasks like incident creation, alert escalation, and response actions.

Threat intelligence: Integrates with threat intelligence feeds for enhanced threat awareness.

Flash Card # 298
What are the benefits of using Azure Sentinel?

Improved security posture: Provides comprehensive visibility into your security landscape and helps detect threats faster.

Reduced risk of breaches: Enables proactive threat hunting and incident response to mitigate potential damage.

Enhanced compliance: Helps meet compliance requirements by providing centralized audit logs and reporting.

Scalability and flexibility: Scales to meet your security needs and integrates with various security tools.

Cost-effectiveness: Offers pay-per-use pricing based on data ingestion volume.

Flash Card # 299
How does Azure Sentinel work?

You configure data connectors to collect security data from different sources.

Sentinel ingests and stores the data in a centralized log repository.

Security analytics and machine learning algorithms analyze the data for anomalies and potential threats.

Alerts are generated for suspicious activity, triggering workflows or requiring manual investigation.

You can use Azure Sentinel for threat hunting, incident response, and security orchestration and automation (SOAR).

Azure Dedicated Host

Flash Card # 300
What is Azure Dedicated Host?

A physical server dedicated to running your Azure virtual machines (VMs) in a specific Azure region. Unlike shared VMs, they provide greater isolation, control, and performance

Flash Card # 301
Who should use Azure Dedicated Hosts?

Organizations requiring strict performance, isolation, control, or compliance needs, those running mission-critical workloads, or needing access to specific hardware features unavailable in standard VMs

Flash Card # 302
What are the benefits of using Azure Dedicated Hosts?

Improved performance: VMs get dedicated physical resources, reducing performance variability and interference.

Enhanced security: Isolated environment reduces the risk of malicious activity from other VMs.

Greater control: Manage and configure hosts directly, including installing custom software or drivers.

Compliance benefits: May meet specific compliance requirements demanding dedicated hardware.

Cost-effective for sustained workloads: Can be cheaper than pay-as-you-go VMs for predictable, consistent usage.

Flash Card # 303
What are the drawbacks of Azure Dedicated Hosts?

Less flexible: Scaling up or down requires provisioning or deprovisioning entire hosts, not individual VMs.

Higher upfront cost: Requires upfront payment for reserved capacity, unlike pay-as-you-go VMs.

Management overhead: Additional effort needed to manage and patch the dedicated hosts.

Flash Card # 304
What are the different types of Azure Dedicated Hosts?

Standard Hosts: General-purpose hosts for most workloads.

Reserved Hosts: Offer significant cost savings through upfront commitment for 1 or 3 years.

Proximity Placement Groups: Hosts co-located within the same physical rack for low-latency connections.

Azure HPC VMs: Hosts optimized for high-performance computing workloads.

Flash Card # 305
How does Azure Dedicated Host enhance compliance?

Azure Dedicated Host allows you to place VMs on servers dedicated exclusively to your organization, helping you meet specific compliance requirements by providing physical isolation from other customers.

Flash Card # 306

What are some best practices for using Azure Dedicated Hosts?

Carefully assess your workload requirements for performance, isolation, and cost before committing.

Choose the right host type based on your specific needs.

Utilize resource groups and tags for organized management.

Implement automation for patching and configuration management.

Monitor host performance and resource utilization.

Privacy, Compliance, and Trust

Flash Card # 307

What are three core principles of a comprehensive approach to Privacy, Compliance, and Trust (PCT)?

Transparency: Clear communication about data practices, collection, and usage.

Accountability: Demonstrating responsible stewardship of data and adhering to regulations

Security: Implementing robust measures to protect data privacy and integrity

Flash Card # 308

What are some key benefits of prioritizing PCT in your organization?

Strengthened customer trust and loyalty, reduced risk of data breaches and fines, improved brand reputation, and smoother business operations

Flash Card # 309

What is the General Data Protection Regulation (GDPR) and how does it impact businesses?

GDPR is a European Union regulation setting high standards for personal data protection and privacy rights, impacting any organization processing EU citizen data.

Flash Card # 310

What are some key compliance frameworks related to PCT?

GDPR, CCPA, HIPAA, PCI DSS, SOC 2, ISO 27001, NIST Cybersecurity Framework

Flash Card # 311

What are some best practices for building a strong PCT foundation?

Conduct regular data privacy impact assessments, implement data governance policies, train employees on privacy practices, use data encryption and access controls, and provide clear privacy notices to users

Flash Card # 312

What role does technology play in supporting PCT?

Privacy-enhancing technologies, security tools, compliance management platforms, and cloud platforms with built-in privacy features can be valuable assets.

Flash Card # 313

How can you build trust with customers regarding data privacy?

Be transparent about your data practices, provide clear opt-in and opt-out choices, respond promptly to privacy inquiries, and demonstrate your commitment to data security.

Flash Card # 314

What are some potential challenges in achieving compliance with PCT regulations?

Keeping up with evolving regulations, managing diverse data sources, balancing privacy with functionality, and addressing employee training needs.

Flash Card # 315

What are some resources for learning more about PCT?

Regulatory websites, industry reports, privacy organizations, online courses, and professional certifications

Secure Azure Resources with RBAC

Flash Card # 316
What is Azure Role-Based Access Control (RBAC)?

A framework for managing access to Azure resources by assigning roles with specific permissions to users, groups, or service principals.

Flash Card # 317
What are the key benefits of using RBAC?

Granular access control, reduced risk of unauthorized access, improved compliance, and simplified security management.

Flash Card # 318
What are the different types of roles in RBAC?

Built-in roles with predefined permissions, custom roles for specific needs, and Azure AD roles for managing identities.

Flash Card # 319
How can you assign roles to users, groups, or service principals?

Through the Azure portal, Azure CLI, Azure PowerShell, or programmatically using APIs

Flash Card # 320
What are some best practices for securing Azure resources with RBAC?

Grant least privilege access (principle of least privilege), use built-in roles when possible, regularly review and update access permissions, monitor access logs, and leverage Azure Active Directory for identity and access management.

Flash Card # 321
What are Azure resource groups and how do they relate to RBAC?

Resource groups organize related Azure resources, and RBAC can be applied at the resource group or individual resource level

Flash Card # 322
How can you manage access to specific resources within a resource group?

Use nested RBAC to assign roles with more granular permissions to specific resources within a group.

Flash Card # 323
What are Azure Management Locks and how can they be used with RBAC?

Management locks prevent accidental deletion or modification of resources, adding an extra layer of security on top of RBAC

Flash Card # 324
How can you audit access to Azure resources?

Use Azure Monitor logs to track resource access attempts, successful and unsuccessful, for auditing and security analysis.

Flash Card # 325
What are Azure tags?

Azure tags are metadata labels applied to Azure resources to help organize and categorize them. Tags consist of name-value pairs and provide a flexible way to add custom information to resources for better management, resource grouping, and cost tracking.

Secure Azure Resources with RBAC

Flash Card # 326
What is the primary purpose of Azure Resource Locks?

To prevent accidental or unauthorized deletion or modification of critical Azure resources

Flash Card # 327
What types of resources can be locked with Azure Resource Locks?

Virtually any Azure resource, including virtual machines, storage accounts, resource groups, subscriptions, and more.

Flash Card # 328
What are the different lock levels available in Azure Resource Locks?

There are two levels: Read-only lock prevents deletion and modification, and Deny all prevents deletion, modification, and any other operations on the resource.

Flash Card # 329
Who can apply and remove Azure Resource Locks?

Users with sufficient permissions (usually owners or administrators) can apply and remove locks.

Flash Card # 330

How can Azure Resource Locks be applied?

Locks can be applied through the Azure portal, Azure CLI, Azure PowerShell, or programmatically using APIs.

Flash Card # 331

What are some best practices for using Azure Resource Locks?

Apply locks selectively to critical resources only.

Use read-only locks when possible to allow essential maintenance.

Document the purpose and duration of each lock.

Review and update locks regularly to ensure they remain relevant.

Communicate lock applications to relevant stakeholders.

Flash Card # 332

What are some potential drawbacks of using Azure Resource Locks?

They can hinder legitimate management activities if not applied carefully.

Removing locks accidentally can leave resources unprotected.

Flash Card # 333

How can Azure Resource Locks be used in conjunction with Azure RBAC?

Back: Resource Locks offer an additional layer of security on top of RBAC by preventing even authorized users from performing certain actions.

Front: What are some alternative or complementary security measures for Azure resources?

Back: Azure Monitor for logging and auditing, Azure Security Center for vulnerability scanning and threat detection, and Azure Policy for enforcing resource configurations.

Flash Card # 334

What are some alternative or complementary security measures for Azure resources?

Azure Monitor for logging and auditing, Azure Security Center for vulnerability scanning and threat detection, and Azure Policy for enforcing resource configurations.

Compliance

Flash Card # 335
What is Compliance?

Adherence to a set of rules, regulations, or standards established by external parties like governments, industries, or professional organizations.

Flash Card # 336
Why is compliance important?

Minimizes legal risks and penalties, protects sensitive data, builds trust with stakeholders, enhances brand reputation, and improves internal processes.

Flash Card # 337
What are some common types of compliance?

Data privacy (GDPR, CCPA), information security (ISO 27001, PCI DSS), financial reporting (SOX), healthcare (HIPAA), and industry-specific regulations.

Flash Card # 338
What are the key steps in achieving compliance?

Identify applicable regulations, assess current state, develop a compliance program, implement controls and procedures, train employees, monitor and audit compliance, and report as required.

Flash Card # 339
What are some challenges in achieving compliance?

Keeping up with evolving regulations, managing diverse data systems, balancing compliance with business needs, and allocating resources effectively.

Flash Card # 340
What are some best practices for staying compliant?

Assign a dedicated compliance officer, conduct regular risk assessments, automate compliance tasks, use compliance management tools, and foster a culture of compliance within the organization.

Flash Card # 341
How can technology help with compliance?

Compliance management platforms, cloud security solutions, data encryption tools, and identity and access management solutions can streamline compliance efforts.

Flash Card # 342
What are some resources for learning more about compliance?

Regulatory websites, industry associations, professional certifications, online courses, and compliance consulting firms.

Azure Government Cloud

Flash Card # 343
What is Azure Government Cloud?

A separate, isolated instance of the Microsoft Azure cloud specifically designed for U.S. government agencies and their partners.

Flash Card # 344
What are the key benefits of using Azure Government Cloud?

Enhanced security: Meets strict government security requirements like FedRAMP High and DoD DISA SRG Impact Level 5.

Data isolation: Physical and logical separation from the public Azure cloud ensures data residency and sovereignty.

Compliance support: Facilitates adherence to regulations like FISMA, HIPAA, and ITAR.

Government-trained personnel: Microsoft employs US-cleared personnel to manage and operate the cloud.

Flash Card # 345
What are some of the limitations of Azure Government Cloud?

Limited service availability: Not all Azure services are currently available in the Gov Cloud.

Higher costs: May have slightly higher pricing compared to the public Azure cloud.

Slower feature updates: New features may roll out with a delay compared to the public cloud.

Flash Card # 346
Who can use Azure Government Cloud?

U.S. federal, state, and local government agencies.

U.S. government contractors and partners working on government projects.

Flash Card # 347
What are some common use cases for Azure Government Cloud?

Building secure cloud applications for government agencies.

Hosting sensitive government data in a compliant environment.

Enabling collaboration between government agencies and partners.

Modernizing legacy IT infrastructure with cloud-based solutions.

Flash Card # 348
How does Azure Government Cloud compare to other government cloud offerings?

AWS GovCloud and Google Cloud Platform (GCP) for Government also offer similar features and capabilities.

Evaluate each platform based on specific needs, security requirements, and budget constraints.

Flash Card # 349

What are some best practices for using Azure Government Cloud?

Thoroughly assess your security and compliance requirements.

Choose the right services and configurations for your specific needs.

Implement strong access controls and data encryption practices.

Regularly monitor and audit your cloud environment for security threats

Azure Privacy

Flash Card # 350
What is Azure Privacy?

A collection of Microsoft's policies, practices, and commitments related to data privacy in the Azure cloud platform

Flash Card # 351
What are some key principles of Azure Privacy?

Transparency, control, security, and compliance with global privacy regulations (e.g., GDPR, CCPA).

Flash Card # 352
What kind of data does Microsoft collect in Azure?

Usage data (resource utilization), customer data (subscription information), diagnostic data (system performance), and content data (user-uploaded files)

Flash Card # 353
How does Microsoft protect user data in Azure?

Encryption at rest and in transit, access controls, regular security audits, and compliance certifications

Flash Card # 354
What controls do you have over my data in Azure?

You can manage data deletion, access logs, and opt-out of certain data collection practices

Flash Card # 355
What are some Azure services with specific privacy features?

Azure Information Protection (classifies and protects sensitive data), Azure Defender (threat detection and incident response), and Azure Active Directory (identity and access management).

Flash Card # 356
How can you learn more about Azure Privacy practices?

Microsoft Privacy Statement, Azure Trust Center, Microsoft Security Documentation, and Azure Data Protection offerings

Flash Card # 357
What are some challenges surrounding Azure Privacy?

Balancing transparency with security needs, understanding complex data collection practices, and navigating different regional privacy regulations.

Flash Card # 358

How can you ensure my organization adheres to privacy regulations in Azure?

Conduct data privacy assessments, implement data governance policies, train employees on privacy practices, and use privacy-enhancing technologies.

Azure Trust

Flash Card # 359
What is Azure Trust?

Microsoft's comprehensive approach to building and maintaining trust in the Azure cloud platform. It encompasses security, privacy, compliance, transparency, and accountability.

Flash Card # 360
What are the pillars of Azure Trust?

Protecting data and infrastructure from unauthorized access, threats, and vulnerabilities.

Privacy: Collecting, using, and storing data responsibly and transparently.

Compliance: Adhering to global and industry-specific regulations and standards.

Transparency: Openly communicating practices, policies, and incidents related to security and privacy.

Accountability: Taking responsibility for the security and privacy of customer data.

Flash Card # 361
What are some key features that demonstrate Azure's commitment to Trust?

Regular independent security audits, certifications by leading standards bodies, transparent incident reporting, and data residency options.

Flash Card # 362
How does Azure Trust benefit users?

Increased confidence in cloud security and data privacy, reduced compliance risks, and improved brand reputation for organizations using Azure.

Flash Card # 363
What are some specific Azure services and tools that contribute to Trust?

Azure Security Center, Azure Sentinel, Azure Active Directory, Azure Information Protection, Azure Attestation, and Microsoft Defender for Cloud.

Flash Card # 364
How can you learn more about Azure Trust?

Microsoft Azure Trust Center, Azure security documentation, compliance documentation, Microsoft Security blog, and Azure community forums.

Flash Card # 365
What are some challenges in maintaining trust in the cloud?

Evolving security threats, complex regulatory landscapes, and balancing transparency with security requirements.

Flash Card # 366

How can organizations leverage Azure Trust to build trust with their customers?

Clearly communicate their commitment to Azure Trust principles, demonstrate compliance with relevant regulations, and be transparent about data practices.

Azure Pricing Factors

Flash Card # 367
What are the main factors that affect Azure pricing?

Resource type, resource consumption, service location, purchase option, and support plan.

Flash Card # 368
How does the chosen resource type affect cost?

Different resources (virtual machines, storage, databases, etc.) have different pricing models based on factors like CPU, memory, storage, and networking capabilities.

Flash Card # 369
How does resource consumption impact cost?

You typically pay for what you use, so higher resource utilization leads to higher costs. Analyze resource usage patterns to optimize costs.

Flash Card # 370
How does the chosen service location affect price?

Prices may vary depending on the Azure region you choose due to factors like data transfer costs and local infrastructure.

Flash Card # 371
What are the different purchase options and how do they influence cost?

Pay-as-you-go is flexible but can be more expensive. Reserved instances offer discounts for committed usage upfront. Enterprise Agreements provide volume discounts.

Flash Card # 372
How does the chosen support plan affect cost?

Basic support is included, but advanced support plans offer faster response times and additional features, resulting in higher costs.

Flash Card # 373
What are some additional factors to consider?

Data transfer costs, egress fees, network charges, and managed service costs can also contribute to your overall Azure bill.

Flash Card # 374
What tools can help me estimate my Azure costs?

Azure Pricing Calculator, Azure Cost Management tools, and spending forecasts in the Azure portal.

Flash Card # 375
How can you optimize my Azure spending?

Right-size resources, utilize reserved instances, leverage spot VMs, automate resource scaling, and monitor resource usage patterns.

Total Cost of Ownership (TCO) Calculator

Flash Card # 376
What is a Total Cost of Ownership (TCO) Calculator?

A tool that helps you estimate the full cost of owning and operating a technology solution, including its acquisition, deployment, management, and support costs.

Flash Card # 377
What are the benefits of using a TCO Calculator for Azure?

Helps compare different deployment options (on-premises, cloud, hybrid), identify cost-saving opportunities, make informed budgeting decisions, and justify cloud investments.

Flash Card # 378
What are the key inputs required for an Azure TCO Calculator?

Specific Azure services you plan to use, estimated usage (e.g., compute hours, storage space), chosen service tiers, deployment region, support plan, and potential on-premises costs you intend to replace.

Flash Card # 379
What are some outputs you can expect from an Azure TCO Calculator?

Breakdown of costs across different categories (acquisition, infrastructure, management, support), total estimated TCO, potential savings compared to on-premises alternatives, and cost optimization recommendations.

Flash Card # 380
Where can you find Azure TCO Calculators?

Microsoft Azure Cost Management tools, online third-party TCO calculators (e.g., Gartner, Forrester), and cloud consulting firms offering TCO assessments.

Flash Card # 381
What limitations should you be aware of when using TCO Calculators?

Outputs are estimates based on assumptions, future costs may change, and hidden costs (e.g., data transfer) might not be fully captured.

Flash Card # 382
How can you improve the accuracy of my TCO estimates?

Gather accurate usage data from existing on-premises systems, consider potential future scaling needs, and refine your assumptions based on real-world usage patterns after deployment.

Flash Card # 383
What else should you consider beyond cost when making a cloud deployment decision?

Security, performance, scalability, vendor lock-in, and integration with existing IT infrastructure are also important factors to evaluate.

Best Practices for Minimizing Azure Costs

Flash Card # 384
Right-size your resources?

Choose the appropriate resource type and configuration (e.g., VM size, storage tier) based on your actual needs. Avoid overprovisioning.

Flash Card # 385
Utilize reserved instances?

Commit to upfront payment for sustained workloads and receive significant discounts compared to pay-as-you-go pricing.

Flash Card # 386
Leverage spot VMs?

Bid on unused Azure capacity for significant cost savings, suitable for fault-tolerant, non-critical workloads.

Flash Card # 387
Automate resource scaling?

Use autoscaling rules to adjust resource usage based on predefined metrics, avoiding unnecessary idle resources.

Flash Card # 388
Monitor resource consumption?

Analyze usage patterns with Azure Cost Management tools to identify opportunities for optimization and cost reduction.

Flash Card # 389
Implement cost allocation tags?

Tag resources with relevant information (department, project) to track costs and identify cost centers.

Flash Card # 390
Take advantage of free Azure tiers?

Utilize free services and quotas offered by Azure for development, testing, and small-scale workloads.

Flash Card # 391
Clean up unused resources?

Regularly identify and remove unused or abandoned resources to prevent unnecessary charges

Flash Card # 392
Consider managed services?

While they may have an upfront cost, managed services can automate tasks and potentially reduce overall costs through efficiency gains.

Flash Card # 393
Negotiate Enterprise Agreements?

For large organizations, negotiate volume discounts and other benefits through Azure Enterprise Agreements

Managing and Deploying Azure Resources

Flash Card # 394

What are some key tools for managing and deploying Azure resources?

Azure portal, Azure Resource Manager (ARM) templates, Azure CLI, Azure PowerShell, Bicep (infrastructure as code), and third-party tools like Terraform.

Flash Card # 395

What are the benefits of using ARM templates for deployments?

Consistent and repeatable deployments, reduced human error, infrastructure version control, and easier collaboration.

Flash Card # 396

What are some best practices for managing Azure resources?

Organize resources using resource groups and tags.

Implement role-based access control (RBAC) for security.

Monitor resource usage and performance.

Automate tasks with Azure Automation or Logic Apps.

Back up critical resources with Azure Backup.

Leverage Azure Cost Management tools for cost optimization

Flash Card # 397

What are some considerations for deploying infrastructure in different Azure regions?

Availability zones, latency, data residency requirements, and pricing differences

Flash Card # 398

How can you ensure high availability of your Azure resources?

Use availability sets, redundant virtual machines, Azure Site Recovery, and load balancers.

Flash Card # 399

What are some strategies for disaster recovery in Azure?

Back up data with Azure Backup, use geo-replication for resources across regions, and leverage Azure Site Recovery for failover.

Flash Card # 400

How can you manage infrastructure changes in Azure?

Use ARM templates and deployment pipelines, implement continuous integration and continuous delivery (CI/CD), and utilize Infrastructure as Code (IaC) tools

Flash Card # 401

What are some key security considerations for managing Azure resources?

Implement strong passwords, use RBAC effectively, encrypt sensitive data, monitor for security threats, and stay updated on security best practices

Azure Resource Manager (ARM)

Flash Card # 402
What is Azure Resource Manager (ARM)?

A service for managing and deploying Azure resources in a consistent and declarative way

Flash Card # 403
What are the benefits of using ARM?

Declarative: Describe what you want, not how to achieve it.

Repeatable: Deploy resources consistently and reliably.

Scalable: Manage large and complex deployments efficiently.

Secure: Control access and permissions with role-based access control (RBAC)

Versionable: Track changes and rollback deployments if needed

Flash Card # 404
What are the key components of an ARM template?

Resources: Define type and properties of each resource to be deployed.

Properties: Specify configuration details for each resource.

Dependencies: Define the order in which resources are deployed.

Parameters: Allow customization of template values during deployment

Flash Card # 405
How can you deploy ARM templates?

Azure portal: Through the Manage deployments feature.

Azure CLI: Using commands like az deployment group create.

Azure PowerShell: Using cmdlets like New-AzResourceGroupDeployment.

REST API: Programmatically deploy templates.

Infrastructure as Code (IaC) tools: Like Terraform or Bicep

Flash Card # 406
What are some best practices for writing ARM templates?

Use modules for reusability and organization.

Leverage variables for customization.

Validate templates for syntax errors.

Use comments to document your templates.

Follow secure coding practices

Flash Card # 407
What are some advanced features of ARM?

Linked templates: Reference other templates for modularity.

Deployment scripts: Execute PowerShell scripts during deployment.

Resource groups: Organize related resources logically.

Managed service identities: Grant resources access to other resources

Structure of ARM Templates

Flash Card # 408
What are the three main sections of an ARM template?

Resources, properties, and dependencies

Flash Card # 409
What defines the type and properties of each resource to be deployed?

The Resources section, with each resource having its own key-value pair structure

Flash Card # 410
What specifies the desired configuration details for each resource?

The Properties section within each resource definition, specifying attributes like VM size, storage capacity, etc

Flash Card # 411
How do you define the order in which resources are deployed?

The DependsOn property within each resource, referencing other resources it relies on

Flash Card # 412
What allows you to customize template values during deployment?

Parameters section, defining variables users can input when deploying the template.

Flash Card # 413
How do you organize reusable resource configurations within templates?

Use Modules section, encapsulating common configurations for later reference.

Flash Card # 414
What helps document your templates and improve readability?

Include Comments section with clear explanations for different parts of the template

Flash Card # 415
How can you validate your template for syntax errors before deployment?

Use online validators or Azure Resource Explorer tool for template verification

Flash Card # 416

What additional sections can you use in advanced ARM templates?

Outputs section for capturing deployment results, Variables section for complex value management, and Linked Templates for referencing other templates for modularity

Working with ARM Templates

Flash Card # 417
How do you create an ARM template?

You can use text editors, Visual Studio Code extensions, or Azure portal tools like "Manage deployments" or "Resource Explorer."

Flash Card # 418
How do you create an ARM template?

You can use text editors, Visual Studio Code extensions, or Azure portal tools like "Manage deployments" or "Resource Explorer."

Flash Card # 419
What tools can help you validate your ARM template?

The Azure portal, online validators, Azure Resource Explorer, and command-line tools like az deployment validate

Flash Card # 420
How do you deploy an ARM template?

You can deploy them through the Azure portal, Azure CLI, Azure PowerShell, REST API, or Infrastructure as Code (IaC) tools like Terraform or Bicep.

Flash Card # 421
What are some best practices for writing ARM templates?

Modularize your code: Use modules for reusability and organization.

Leverage variables: Allow customization of template values during deployment.

Validate and test your templates: Ensure syntax accuracy and desired behavior.

Document your templates: Use comments to explain configurations.

Follow secure coding practices: Avoid hardcoding secrets and use managed identities.

Flash Card # 422
What are some advanced features you can use in ARM templates?

Linked templates: Reference other templates for modularity.

Deployment scripts: Execute PowerShell scripts during deployment.

Resource groups: Organize related resources logically.

Managed service identities: Grant resources access to other resources.

Conditional statements and loops: Control resource creation based on conditions.

Flash Card # 423
How can you manage different versions of your ARM templates?

Use version control systems like Git.

Leverage Azure Resource Manager deployment history.

Implement CI/CD pipelines for automated deployments

Azure Arc

Flash Card # 424
What types of resources can be managed with Azure Arc?

Servers: Windows and Linux virtual machines and physical servers.

Kubernetes clusters: Manage Kubernetes clusters anywhere.

Databases: Manage SQL Server, PostgreSQL, and MySQL databases.

Applications: Deploy and manage containerized applications

Flash Card # 425
What are the core components of Azure Arc?

Azure Arc enabled resources: Resources registered with Azure and managed through Azure services.

Azure Arc data plane: Agents deployed on resources for communication and management.

Azure Arc control plane: Services in Azure for centralized management and governance.

Flash Card # 426
What are some security considerations for using Azure Arc?

Implement role-based access control (RBAC) for secure access.

Use Azure Defender for enhanced threat detection and protection.

Securely connect your on-premises environment to Azure

Flash Card # 427
How can you get started with Azure Arc?

Register your resources with Azure Arc.

Choose the appropriate management tools and services based on your needs.

Leverage Azure learning resources and documentation for further guidance

Flash Card # 428
What are some real-world use cases for Azure Arc?

Modernizing legacy applications by migrating them to Kubernetes.

Managing on-premises databases with consistent policies and governance.

Gaining visibility and control over edge computing deployments

Flash Card # 429
How does Azure Arc compare to other hybrid cloud management solutions?

Evaluate factors like supported resources, management tools, pricing models, and security features

Azure Portal

Flash Card # 430
What are the key features of the Azure Portal?

Resource management: Create, view, update, and delete Azure resources.

Monitoring and diagnostics: Monitor resource health, performance, and troubleshoot issues.

Billing and cost management: Track your Azure spending and optimize costs.

Security and compliance: Manage user access, configure security policies, and ensure compliance.

Automation and tools: Automate tasks with Azure Automation and leverage various tools for development and management

Flash Card # 431
How do you navigate the Azure Portal?

Use the search bar, browse by category, or utilize the resource groups for organization.

Flash Card # 432
What are some personalization options in the Azure Portal?

Customize the dashboard, create custom shortcuts, and set favorite resources for quick access.

Flash Card # 433
How can you manage different subscriptions in the Azure Portal?

Switch between subscriptions easily and manage access permissions for each.

Flash Card # 434
What are some security best practices for using the Azure Portal?

Enable multi-factor authentication, use strong passwords, and avoid sharing credentials.

Flash Card # 435
What are some advanced features of the Azure Portal?

Use Azure Resource Manager (ARM) templates for deployment, leverage Azure Policy for governance, and explore Azure Monitor for in-depth insights.

Flash Card # 436
How can you learn more about using the Azure Portal?

Microsoft Azure documentation: https://learn.microsoft.com/en-us/azure/

Azure Portal learning path: https://learn.microsoft.com/en-us/azure/azure-portal/

Azure blog posts and community forums.

Flash Card # 437

What are some helpful keyboard shortcuts for navigating the Azure Portal?

Learn essential shortcuts for faster navigation and increased efficiency.

Azure Plan

Flash Card # 438
What is Azure Plan?

A subscription offering in Azure that combines services and management features into a predictable monthly cost.

Flash Card # 439
What are the different types of Azure Plans?

Individual Plans, Developer Plans, and Enterprise Agreement Plans, each with varying resource limits and features.

Flash Card # 440
What are the benefits of using Azure Plan?

Predictable costs: Know your monthly bill upfront, aiding budgeting and cost control.

Simplified management: Reduce complexity with pre-configured resources and management tools.

Improved resource utilization: Leverage included benefits like Azure credits and DevTest Labs environments.

Access to additional features: Some plans offer exclusive features like reserved instance discounts or extended support hours.

Flash Card # 441
What are some limitations of Azure Plan?

Less flexibility than pay-as-you-go options.

Resource limits within each plan cannot be exceeded.

May not be suitable for highly variable workloads or unpredictable usage patterns

Flash Card # 442
What are some key considerations when choosing an Azure Plan?

Your expected resource usage: Estimate your resource needs to choose a plan with adequate capacity.

Desired features: Select a plan offering the features and benefits you require.

Budget constraints: Compare plan costs and ensure they fit your budget.

Flash Card # 443
How can you monitor my Azure Plan usage?

Use the Azure Cost Management tools to track resource consumption and optimize spending within your plan.

Flash Card # 444
What happens when you exceed the resource limits of my Azure Plan?

You will be charged additional fees for exceeding included resources. Consider upgrading your plan or optimizing resource usage to avoid excess costs.

Flash Card # 445
Can you switch between Azure Plans?

Yes, you can upgrade or downgrade plans based on your evolving needs, but switching may incur charges.

Flash Card # 446
What are some alternatives to Azure Plans?

Pay-as-you-go pricing, reserved instances, and Enterprise Agreements offer different cost models and flexibility.

Service Level Agreements (SLAs) in Azure

Flash Card # 447
What is a Service Level Agreement (SLA)?

A formal agreement between a cloud provider (e.g., Microsoft) and a customer that defines the expected performance, availability, and support levels for a specific service.

Flash Card # 448
What are the key components of an SLA in Azure?

Service definitions: The specific Azure services covered by the agreement.

Availability commitment: The guaranteed uptime percentage for the service.

Performance metrics: Measurable indicators like latency, throughput, and response times.

Financial remedies: Service credits or discounts offered for SLA breaches.

Support response times: Guaranteed response times for technical issues

Flash Card # 449
What are the different types of SLAs offered by Azure?

Basic support SLA: Included with all Azure subscriptions, offers basic support features but lower financial remedies.

Standard support SLA: Paid tier offering faster response times and higher financial remedies.

Premium support SLA: Top-tier offering with the fastest response times, proactive monitoring, and dedicated engineers.

Flash Card # 450
What are some additional benefits of having an SLA in Azure?

Increased trust and transparency: Provides clear expectations and accountability.

Improved budgeting and planning: Predictable costs associated with service disruptions.

Enhanced risk mitigation: Defines resolution procedures for service issues.

Flash Card # 451
What are some limitations of SLAs in Azure?

Not all services have an SLA.

SLAs may not cover all potential issues.

Financial remedies may not fully compensate for downtime or performance issues.

Flash Card # 452
How can you find the SLA for a specific Azure service?

Access the service documentation on the Microsoft Azure website.

Look for the "Service Level Agreements" section within the documentation.

Alternatively, search for the service name and "SLA" on the Azure website.

Flash Card # 453
What should you do if you experience an SLA breach in Azure?

Contact Azure support and reference the specific SLA terms.

Provide detailed information about the issue and its impact.

Work with Azure support to resolve the issue and claim any applicable financial remedies

Flash Card # 454
How can you use SLAs to make informed decisions about Azure services?

Compare SLAs of different services to select the one that best meets your needs.

Use SLAs to assess the potential risks and financial implications of service disruptions.

Consider SLAs alongside other factors like pricing, features, and your risk tolerance

Azure Authentication

Flash Card # 455
What are the main methods of authentication in Azure?

Azure Active Directory (AD) password-based authentication, multi-factor authentication (MFA), Azure AD single sign-on (SSO), social logins, and certificate-based authentication.

Flash Card # 456
What is Azure AD password-based authentication?

Traditional username and password login for accessing Azure resources and applications

Flash Card # 457
What is Azure AD Multi-Factor Authentication (MFA)?

Adds an extra layer of security by requiring a secondary verification factor, like a phone call or code, upon login

Flash Card # 458
What are the benefits of using Azure AD single sign-on (SSO)?

Allows users to sign in once for multiple applications, improving convenience and security.

Flash Card # 459
What are social logins in Azure AD?

Enables users to log in to Azure applications using their existing social media credentials (e.g., Facebook, Google)

Flash Card # 460
What is certificate-based authentication in Azure?

Uses digital certificates for secure access to Azure resources, often used for server-to-server communication.

Flash Card # 461
What are the key components of Azure AD for authentication?

Users, groups, applications, access policies, and conditional access rules.

Flash Card # 462
What are conditional access rules in Azure AD?

Define security requirements for accessing Azure resources based on factors like device, location, or application.

Flash Card # 463
What are some best practices for securing Azure authentication?

Use strong passwords, enforce MFA, implement conditional access policies, and regularly review user access permissions.

Flash Card # 464
How can you manage Azure AD authentication for my organization?

Use the Azure portal, Azure PowerShell, Azure CLI, or tools like Microsoft Intune.

Flash Card # 465
What are some resources for learning more about Azure authentication?

Microsoft Azure documentation, Azure AD learning path, Azure security documentation, and online tutorials.

Flash Card # 466
What are the emerging trends in Azure authentication?

Passwordless authentication, biometrics, and adaptive authentication based on user behavior and risk factors.

Azure Cloud Shell

Flash Card # 467
What is Azure Cloud Shell?

A browser-based, managed command-line environment for interacting with Azure resources directly within your web browser.

Flash Card # 468
What are the key benefits of using Azure Cloud Shell?

Accessible from anywhere: No need to install software, works on any device with a web browser.

Pre-configured environment: Includes Azure CLI, PowerShell, and common tools for Azure management.

Integrated with Azure portal: Seamless access to your subscriptions and resources.

Secure and ephemeral: Runs in a temporary environment, enhancing security and consistency.

Multiple shell options: Choose between Bash, PowerShell, and Cloud Shell 2.0 (Windows PowerShell).

Flash Card # 469
How can you access Azure Cloud Shell?

Directly from the Azure portal, the Azure CLI, or a browser bookmark.

Flash Card # 470

What features does Azure Cloud Shell offer?

File editing: Edit and manage files directly within the shell environment.

Code completion: Get suggestions for commands and parameters as you type.

Syntax highlighting: Improves readability and helps identify errors.

Customizations: Set preferences for fonts, themes, and keyboard shortcuts.

Integrations: Work with other Azure services and tools directly from the shell.

Flash Card # 471

What are some security considerations when using Azure Cloud Shell?

Be mindful of commands you run: Avoid executing potentially risky commands.

Use multi-factor authentication: Add an extra layer of security to your login.

Don't store sensitive information directly in the shell: Use secure storage mechanisms for secrets.

Flash Card # 472

What are some real-world use cases for Azure Cloud Shell?

Managing Azure resources from anywhere, without local software installation.

Scripting and automating tasks within the Azure environment.

Troubleshooting and diagnosing issues with Azure resources.

Learning and exploring Azure services through direct command-line interaction

Flash Card # 473

What are the differences between Azure Cloud Shell and other command-line tools like Azure CLI or PowerShell?

Cloud Shell provides a pre-configured, browser-based environment, while CLI and PowerShell require local installation and configuration.

Azure PowerShell

Flash Card # 474
How do you get started with Azure PowerShell?

Install the Az modules: Install-Module -Name Az

Connect to your Azure subscription: Connect-AzAccount

Explore available cmdlets: Get-AzCommand

Flash Card # 475
What are some basic Azure PowerShell cmdlets?

Get resources: Get-AzResource, Get-AzVM

Create resources: New-AzResourceGroup, New-AzVM

Update resources: Set-AzResource, Update-AzVM

Delete resources: Remove-AzResource, Remove-AzVM.

Flash Card # 476
What are some advanced features of Azure PowerShell?

Use Azure Resource Manager (ARM) templates for deployment.

Leverage Azure Policy for governance and compliance.

Integrate with Azure Monitor for resource insights and diagnostics.

Use modules for reusable code and organization.

Flash Card # 477
What are some best practices for writing Azure PowerShell scripts?

Use clear and concise code with comments.

Follow security best practices like using secrets securely.

Test your scripts thoroughly before deployment.

Use error handling and logging effectively.

Flash Card # 478
What are some real-world use cases for Azure PowerShell?

Automating Azure resource deployments and configuration.

Managing large-scale infrastructure environments.

Integrating with DevOps pipelines for CI/CD.

Scripting complex tasks for Azure resource management.

Flash Card # 479
How does Azure PowerShell compare to other Azure management tools like Azure CLI?

Both offer similar functionalities, but PowerShell offers more scripting capabilities and integrates better with existing Windows environments.

Azure Identity Services

Flash Card # 480
What are the core Azure Identity Services?

Azure Active Directory (AD), Azure AD Multi-Factor Authentication (MFA), Azure AD Identity Protection, and Azure Managed Identities.

Flash Card # 481
How does Azure AD Multi-Factor Authentication (MFA) enhance security?

Adds an extra layer of verification beyond passwords, preventing unauthorized access attempts.

Flash Card # 482
What does Azure AD Identity Protection offer?

Advanced threat protection features like risk detection, conditional access, and identity governance.

Flash Card # 483
What is the benefit of using Azure Managed Identities?

Simplify application access to Azure resources without manually managing credentials.

Flash Card # 484
What are some key features of Azure Active Directory?

User and group management: Manage users, groups, and their permissions.

Application registration and access: Register and grant access to various applications.

Single Sign-On (SSO): Access multiple applications with one login.

Directory synchronization: Synchronize on-premises identities with Azure AD.

Flash Card # 485
What are some benefits of using Azure AD MFA?

Reduced risk of credential breaches: Difficult for attackers to bypass second-factor verification.

Comply with security regulations: Meets various compliance requirements.

Increased user confidence: Provides stronger security posture.

Flash Card # 486
What does Azure AD Identity Protection provide?

Risk detection and mitigation: Identifies and blocks suspicious activity.

Conditional access: Enforces access policies based on factors like location and device.

Identity governance: Provides insights and controls for managing identities.

Flash Card # 487
How do Azure Managed Identities work?

Assigned to Azure resources like VMs or apps.

Automatically acquire access tokens for Azure resources without needing user credentials.

Simplify security and reduce credential management overhead.

Flash Card # 488
What are some scenarios where Azure Identity Services are valuable?

Securing access to cloud resources for employees and external users.

Implementing multi-factor authentication for enhanced security.

Meeting compliance requirements with advanced identity protection features.

Simplifying application access management with Managed Identities.

Flash Card # 489
How should you choose the right Azure Identity Services for your needs?

Consider factors like security requirements, application types, user access needs, and budget.

Flash Card # 490
What are the key components of AVD?

Host pools: Collections of virtual machines (VMs) hosting desktops and applications.

Session hosts: Individual VMs within a host pool assigned to users.

Desktop and app groups: Define which desktops and applications users can access.

Front-end infrastructure: Web, mobile, and thin client access points.

Flash Card # 491
What are the benefits of using AVD?

Simplified management: Manage desktops and applications centrally in the cloud.

Security: Leverage Azure security features and access control.

Scalability: Easily scale desktops and applications up or down based on demand.

Accessibility: Access desktops from any device with internet connectivity.

Reduced costs: Pay only for the resources you use.

Flash Card # 492
What are some deployment options for AVD?

Bring your own license (BYOL): Use existing Windows licenses with AVD.

Pay-as-you-go: No upfront costs, pay per user per hour.

Front: What are some considerations when deploying AVD?

User needs: Determine desktop and application requirements.

Performance: Choose appropriate VM sizes and network configuration.

Security: Implement access control and data security measures.

Cost: Evaluate BYOL vs. pay-as-you-go options.

Flash Card # 493
How can you integrate AVD with other Azure services?

AVD integrates with various services like Azure Active Directory, Azure Monitor, and Azure Files for identity management, monitoring, and file storage, respectively.

Traffic Manager and Azure DNS

Flash Card # 494
What is Azure Traffic Manager?

A load balancing service that distributes incoming traffic across multiple endpoints based on routing rules and health checks.

Flash Card # 495
What types of endpoints can Traffic Manager work with?

Azure endpoints (VMs, App Services), external endpoints (websites, services), and nested Traffic Manager profiles for multi-level routing.

Flash Card # 496
What routing methods does Traffic Manager offer?

Priority, weighted, geographic, performance-based, and multi-endpoint routing.

Flash Card # 497
What are the benefits of using Traffic Manager?

High availability: Distributes traffic to healthy endpoints, minimizing downtime.

Performance optimization: Routes traffic to the closest or fastest endpoint.

Scalability: Handles surges in traffic effectively.

Load balancing: Distributes traffic evenly across endpoints.

Flash Card # 498
What are some limitations of Traffic Manager?

Not a replacement for application-level load balancing.

Limited customization options compared to some advanced load balancers.

Flash Card # 499
How does Azure DNS enhance security for domain names?

Azure DNS supports DNS Security Extensions (DNSSEC), which helps protect against DNS spoofing and man-in-the-middle attacks by providing data integrity and authentication.

Flash Card # 500
What is the purpose of Azure DNS Private Zones?

Azure DNS Private Zones enables you to host DNS domains in Azure, providing name resolution within your virtual network without exposing DNS entries to the public internet.

Flash Card # 501
How can you integrate Azure DNS with your existing domain registrar?

To use Azure DNS with an existing domain, you need to update your domain registrar's DNS settings to point to Azure DNS name servers. This allows Azure DNS to manage your DNS records.

Flash Card # 502
What types of DNS records does Azure DNS support?

A, AAAA, CNAME, PTR, MX, TXT, and custom records.

About Our Products

Other products from IPSpecialist LTD regarding CSP technology are:

 AWS Certified Cloud Practitioner Study guide

 AWS Certified SysOps Admin - Associate Study guide

 AWS Certified Solution Architect - Associate Study guide

 AWS Certified Developer Associate Study guide

 AWS Certified Advanced Networking – Specialty Study guide

 AWS Certified Security – Specialty Study guide

 AWS Certified Big Data – Specialty Study guide

 Microsoft Certified: Azure Fundamentals

 Microsoft Certified: Azure Administrator

 Microsoft Certified: Azure Solution Architect

 Microsoft Certified: Azure DevOps Engineer

 Microsoft Certified: Azure Developer Associate

 Microsoft Certified: Azure Security Engineer

 Microsoft Certified: Azure Data Fundamentals

 Microsoft Certified: Azure AI Fundamentals

 Microsoft Certified: Azure Data Engineer Associate

 Microsoft Certified: Azure Data Scientist

 Microsoft Certified: Azure Network Engineer

 Oracle Certified: Foundations Associate

Other Network & Security related products from IPSpecialist LTD are:

- Certified Cisco Network Associate Study Guide
- CCNA Routing & Switching Study Guide
- CCNA Security Second Edition Study Guide
- CCNA Service Provider Study Guide
- CCDA Study Guide

- CCDP Study Guide
- CCNP Route Study Guide
- CCNP Switch Study Guide
- CCNP Troubleshoot Study Guide
- CCNP Security SENSS Study Guide
- CCNP Security SIMOS Study Guide
- CCNP Security SITCS Study Guide
- CCNP Security SISAS Study Guide
- CompTIA Network+ Study Guide
- Certified Blockchain Expert (CBEv2) Study Guide
- Ethical Hacking Certification v12 Second Edition Study Guide
- Certified Blockchain Expert v2 Study Guide
- Fortinet Certified Associate in Cybersecurity
- Fortinet FortiOS Study Guide
- Palo Alto Certified Network Security Administrator
- Palo Alto Certified Network Security Engineer

www.ingramcontent.com/pod-product-compliance
Lightning Source LLC
LaVergne TN
LVHW081339050326
832903LV00024B/1224